Praise for *Becoming the Best*

"*Becoming the Best* is both brilliant and powerful. Harry Kraemer recognizes the importance of values-based leadership and provides a focused and insightful how-to primer. He captures the relevance of five often overlooked intangibles that make leadership effective at any level. If you only have time to read one book on leadership, this book is for you."

—Lieutenant General (Ret.) Franklin L. "Buster" Hagenbeck,
Retired Superintendent, U.S. Military Academy, West Point

"With *Becoming the Best*, Harry Kraemer has produced another compelling and insightful addition to the leadership literature. He is not only an accomplished businessman and teacher, he is also a wonderful writer."

—Morton Shapiro,
Professor and President, Northwestern University

"Harry Kraemer has done it again. While management is primarily a business skill, leadership is primarily a human skill—a profoundly human endeavor, in fact, because the most powerful manifestations of leadership occur when we link our day-to-day business activities and behaviors to our overall life values and goals. Once again Harry is shedding light on this challenging trail so that more of us can put on our hiking boots and backpacks and begin or continue this wonderful journey."

—Kent Thiry,
Chairman and CEO, DaVita Inc.

"An award-winning teacher and inspirational leader, Harry Kraemer provides a unique and powerful approach to leadership grounded in the practice of self-reflection and self-knowledge. *Becoming the Best* is an essential guide for all who aspire to become more authentic and impactful leaders."

—Daniel Diermeier,
Dean, Harris School of Public Policy, The University of Chicago

"*Becoming the Best* builds on Harry Kraemer's principles of values-based leadership and offers a practical way to apply these values to one's self, to one's team, and beyond. Often this type of advice is most anxiously consumed by those starting out in their careers who look to an experienced CEO and leader like Harry to help show them the right path. But the real value of this book is for current CEOs and others already in leadership positions who also value advice on how to improve their performance. Often, those of us in leadership positions don't get that feedback from our colleagues. *Becoming the Best* helps fill that critical gap."

—**Jonathan Spector**,
President & CEO, The Conference Board

"Harry Kraemer is my go-to expert on organizational leadership. There is no one speaking or writing today who has a firmer fix on what it takes and what it means to be a values-based leader. He is self-reflective, properly balanced in perspective, and always guided by true self-confidence and genuine humility. He has made a difference in how executives better understanding the nature of leadership, and I fully expect *Becoming the Best* will make a difference in how organizations are led into the challenging future that we all face."

—**James Kristie**,
Editor and Associate Publisher, Directors & Boards

"*Becoming the Best* provides a compelling combination of aspirational goals and practical advice, valuable at any point in a career. The book reminds us that values-based leadership creates organizations that truly excel on all levels including shareholder return. In each chapter Kraemer's advice and real-world examples challenged me to improve my own leadership style and team skills."

—**Mark Burstein,**
President, Lawrence University of Wisconsin

BECOMING THE BEST

BUILD A WORLD-CLASS ORGANIZATION THROUGH **VALUES-BASED LEADERSHIP**

HARRY M. JANSEN KRAEMER JR.

WILEY

To my colleagues from Baxter International—American Hospital Supply, Caremark, Edwards Lifesciences, Allegiance—and Madison Dearborn Partners who taught me what it really means to be a values-based leader.

To my classmates from Abington Heights School in Clarks Summit, Pennsylvania, Lawrence University, and Northwestern University's Kellogg School of Management, who have joined me on the leadership journey.

To my spiritual advisor, Father Edward Sthokal, S.J., leader of the Demontreville Jesuit Retreat House, who for 30 years has taught me the benefit of silent self-reflection and prayer.

To my parents, the late Harry and Patricia Kraemer, who built the foundation of my values.

To my wife, Julie Jansen Kraemer, who by her love and example encourages me to be my best self.

To my children, Suzie, Andrew, Shannon, Diane, and Daniel, who will forever be my best team.

CONTENTS

Introduction: From Four Principles to Five Bests   *1*

SECTION ONE
BEST SELF   11

1 THE SELF-REFLECTIVE, BALANCED LEADER   15
2 THE HUMBLE, SELF-CONFIDENT LEADER   33

SECTION TWO
BEST TEAM   49

3 TURNING AROUND A TEAM   55
4 CREATING A BEST TEAM FROM SCRATCH   73

SECTION THREE
BEST PARTNER   91

5 SUPPLIERS AS BEST PARTNERS: A HOLISTIC   97
  RELATIONSHIP
6 BUILDING BEST-PARTNER CUSTOMER   113
  RELATIONSHIPS

SECTION FOUR
BEST INVESTMENT

131

7 MAKING A BEST INVESTMENT IN TALENT   135
8 THE PROOF POINT: SHAREHOLDER VALUE   151

SECTION FIVE
BEST CITIZEN

167

9 VALUES IN ACTION   171
10 LIVING THE LEGACY AND LEAVING A GLOBAL   185
    FOOTPRINT

Acknowledgments   *201*
About the Author   *205*
Index   *207*

INTRODUCTION: FROM FOUR PRINCIPLES TO FIVE BESTS

O ver the past four years, since the publication of my previous book, *From Values to Action: The Four Principles of Values-Based Leadership,* I have spoken to more than 500 groups across the United States, Latin America, Europe, and Asia. With every audience—whether business, government, spiritual, or academic—I encountered a strong desire to learn more about values-based leadership, which is founded on four principles:

1. **Self-Reflection:** The ability to identify and reflect on what you stand for, what your values are, and what matters most.
2. **Balance:** The ability to see situations from multiple perspectives, including differing viewpoints, to gain a holistic understanding.
3. **True Self-Confidence:** Acceptance of yourself, recognizing your strengths and skill mastery, as well as your weaknesses, while focusing on continuous improvement.
4. **Genuine Humility:** Never forgetting who you are, appreciating the unique value of each person in the organization, and treating everyone with respect.

The more people grasped these principles, the more they wanted to know how, in practical terms, to apply them in their daily lives. From CEOs to first-time managers to students, people want to know what they need to do to make a difference in their organizations and beyond. They came to realize that leadership does not have anything to do with titles and organizational charts. Rather, it has everything to do with the ability to influence others by relating authentically to every individual with whom they come in contact.

People at every level and with any job title, from the newest team members to the CEO, can and should become values-based leaders. Whether someone is the CEO of a company that employs 100,000 people or an entry-level person who just graduated from college, values-based leadership begins with one's ability to understand one's self. Self-knowledge and self-awareness must come first, before someone is able to relate to and influence others in positive and meaningful ways.

For many, becoming more self-aware requires a significant change in mindset. To illustrate, I use the analogy of wanting to become healthier. When people read a compelling book or hear an expert speak on the importance of a healthy lifestyle, they set a goal for themselves to lose weight or start an exercise program. This instantly raises some very practical questions: Where do I start and what do I do? Does being healthy mean I have to exercise excessively or that I can never eat another chocolate bar for the rest of my life? What lasting changes do I need to adopt that will help me reach my goal of being healthier?

Similarly, when people commit to becoming values-based leaders, they want to know exactly what they can do to catalyze change, drive results, and make things happen. People want to understand what it means to lead and influence others, and to do the right thing as defined by their personal values, as well as the mission, vision, and values of their organization. They want to know where to start and what to do, knowing that this is not a fad or a quick fix (like a crash diet), but rather a fundamental change in philosophy, attitude, and behavior (like adopting a healthy lifestyle).

Fortunately, values-based leaders have an invaluable tool at the ready: self-reflection, which is the core principle of values-based leadership. Whenever I address a group, the questions I'm asked most frequently relate to self-reflection and, specifically, how to practice it. People from college students to CEOs want to become more self-reflective in their daily lives. They know intuitively that by gaining greater self-knowledge, they will be better able to lead themselves first, which will then enable them to be more effective in leading others.

As will be discussed further in this book, the benefits of self-reflection are realized through regular (ideally daily) practice, using questions such as: *What did I say I would do today? What am I proud of, and not proud of? How did I lead others and follow others? If I had today to do over again, what would I change? If I am fortunate to have tomorrow, given what I've learned today, how will I act?* Self-reflection may be practiced at the end of the day, or be incorporated into any personal time for introspection, such as taking a walk, going for a jog, or sitting quietly for 15 or 20 minutes. Having practiced self-reflection for all of my adult life, including as CEO of Baxter International, a global health-care company with 50,000 team members (I prefer this term over *employees*), I can attest to the positive results of engaging in this discipline.

Other commonly asked questions include: *How do I develop a balanced perspective? How do I become truly self-confident? How can I gain true self-confidence without being perceived as arrogant or selfish? What does genuine humility really mean? If I am genuinely humble, will I run the risk of not being noticed or being passed over? Do I need both true self-confidence and genuine humility?*

Because of these questions and more, I decided to write this book as a *how-to* on values-based leadership. In addition, many of my students at Northwestern University's Kellogg School of Management have asked me to take the values-based leadership journey to the next level. Since I always listen to my Kellogg students, there was really no alternative for me but to do so!

My first book, *From Values to Action*, stemmed directly from my values-based leadership classes at Kellogg, where I have taught for

10 years. In 2004, I stepped down from my role as chairman and CEO of Baxter International, where I had worked for 22 years, including the last six as CEO. At that time, I was asked by Don Jacobs, Dean Emeritus of Kellogg, to teach at the graduate school. I was surprised by his request, since I'm not an academic with a PhD, but he reminded me (half joking, half serious) of my promise that I would do anything for my graduate school alma mater. Of course, I said yes.

Being a former chief financial officer and having majored in finance at Kellogg, I first considered teaching finance classes. However, based on my 35 years of business experience, I realized I could add more value to the students by teaching leadership. Since then I have taught values-based leadership, which has become one of the most popular classes at Kellogg, because of the keen interest in the topic and a host of talented leaders who, as guest lecturers, share insights from their careers with my students.

One of those students, Samir Gokhale, audio taped all of my values-based leadership lectures and transcribed them in order to convince me to write my first book. His efforts jumpstarted my writing of *From Values to Action* and my speaking about values-based leadership, both of which have been beneficial to my teaching (a virtuous cycle, indeed). In my opinion, you can't truly understand a topic until you have listened intently to others' questions and explained concepts clearly.

Today, I am responding to the questions I receive as part of my speeches and presentations to audiences of every type and description. Over the past four years (and counting) of giving more than eight talks per month, I have met countless people who want to understand how to put the principles of values-based leadership into practice. They are CEOs and other C-level corporate officers, executive managers, middle managers, entry-level individuals, and students. My audiences have included multinational companies such as Google, Aon, McDonald's, Raytheon, AT&T, Target Corporation, Abbott Laboratories, CareerBuilder, and Hospira; universities, including Northwestern, University of Chicago, University of

Notre Dame, University of California, University of Minnesota, and Lawrence University (my undergraduate alma mater); consulting and financial services firms, such as McKinsey & Co., Booz & Company, Accenture, JPMorgan Chase, Bank of Montreal, Ernst & Young, KPMG, Deloitte, Spencer Stuart, and Huron Consulting; smaller startup companies in industries such as software, manufacturing, hospitality, and health care; associations for chief financial officers, chief marketing officers, senior human resources officers, and chief information officers; spiritual leaders, including priests, ministers, and rabbis; and philanthropic and religious/spiritual institutions of all sizes. I also had the opportunity to deliver a TEDx talk on values-based leadership at the United Nations in New York City.

Conceptually, values-based leadership is founded on the four principles of self-reflection, balance, true self-confidence, and genuine humility. On a personal level, these principles become the basis of intentional actions and deep commitments that enable each person at every level of an organization to bring his or her best self to work. At an organizational level, these four principles, when applied, enable the creation of a values-based organization.

In these pages, I give both explanations and concrete examples, drawing from my own experiences, and my interactions with leaders at every level. I include interviews with 10 values-based leaders from diverse organizations, ranging from small to large, private to public, for-profit to not-for-profit, and domestic to global. This book lays out a pathway from understanding the four principles to putting them into practice in what I believe are five key areas that define what it means to be a values-based leader and build a world-class organization. They are:

1. **Best Self:** You actualize who you are meant to become with fuller self-knowledge and a deeper understanding that in order to positively influence and lead people, you first need to relate to them.

2. **Best Team:** All team members understand and appreciate what they're doing, why they're doing it, and how that fits with and fulfills the goals and objectives of the organization.

3. **Best Partner:** The organization and its vendors and suppliers forge a partnership in order to enhance the customer experience. Each party understands what the organization is trying to do and why, as it provides products and/or services.

4. **Best Investment:** Everyone in the organization focuses on generating a return for the owners (whether stockholders, debt holders, a foundation, or other stakeholders) through positive and meaningful actions that support the mission, vision, and values of the organization. As a best investment, an enterprise also commits to developing its greatest asset—the talented team members at every level of the organization. The "hard numbers" of best investment are also the proof points that values-based leadership truly does elevate performance over the long term.

5. **Best Citizen:** From the C-suite to the most junior levels of the organization, everyone is focused not only on success, but also significance, through social responsibility and making a difference in the world, beyond the organization and its people. Beyond philanthropy for charity's sake, best citizenship embraces a broader purpose in what we think of as social responsibility.

Each of these *bests* connects to the others in a holistic structure that elevates the organization, its people, and its purpose. This book mirrors the structure with five interconnected sections, building on the firm foundation of the four principles of values-based leadership.

In Section One, we begin with the individual and becoming your best self as you practice self-reflection to identify your values and commit to act in accordance with them. In this section, we also look at how self-reflection is a valuable tool for developing a balanced perspective, making decisions aligned with one's values, and focusing on what is most important. Two additional components of being your best self are achieving true self-confidence and genuine humility, which are extremely complementary. Working in tandem, these two principles allow you to acknowledge what you know and what you don't, and to value each person with whom you interact.

In Section Two, we broaden our scope from the individual to the collective, with the best team. In the values-based organization, every team member is able to link what he or she does to the overall goals and objectives of the organization. They know that what they do truly matters, and so they commit to doing their best. Developing a best team will be examined in two different contexts: first, turning around a dysfunctional environment and, second, in a fast-paced startup where roles and responsibilities are demanding and fluid.

In Section Three, we widen our perspective outside the organization to become a best partner with suppliers and vendors in order to enhance the customer experience and create value for all. An organization that is a best partner moves beyond financial transactions with customers, and focuses on making customer satisfaction a priority. Within the organization, every department and team—including those that are removed from direct customer interface—are able to link what they do with creating a meaningful customer experience.

Section Four examines what it means to be a best investment, with returns that are measured in more than monetary terms. Being a best investment applies to all organizations—large and small, public and private, corporations and nonprofits—with accountability to stakeholders who want to see evidence that organizational values are being put into action in pursuit of a meaningful return. This section will address the steward leader, who uses self-reflection to examine how team members are motivated and rewarded. In addition, discussion will address team members who need to know if their organization fits their values—and what they can do about it.

The book culminates in Section Five with becoming a best citizen. Part of the mission of both the values-based leader and the values-based organization is to set a standard as a best citizen, making a difference in the local community and in the world. This section will address social responsibility to further the priorities and initiatives that are truly meaningful to the organization and its team members. When an organization is a best citizen, it also encourages people to be their best selves, while developing best teams and best partners, and becoming a best investment—the ultimate win/win. It is a powerful legacy that is both highly personal and yet extends beyond the efforts or ego of any one person.

* * *

The need and desire to become the best through values-based leadership have never been stronger or more critical. Organizations today—large or small, public or private—are confronted with ethical issues, which may result from changes in regulations or uncertainty around where the legal, moral, and ethnical boundaries lie. Large, global organizations face the challenges of operating within a varied tapestry of multiple markets, regions, and countries with unique legal systems and regulations. Even smaller organizations focused on a single market or region must navigate a competitive landscape marked by gray areas that are open to interpretation. Within these complexities, and given the serious consequences of making an error in judgment, values-based leadership is the only way to operate. When a problem arises, it is crucial that individuals at all levels of the organization adopt a values-based leadership approach. That means they are committed to doing the right thing at all times—and doing the best they can do.

Values-based leadership is more than just a defensive playbook for how to respond when a dilemma, problem, or crisis arises. It is a way of thinking, acting, and operating at every level of the organization. We cannot merely look at the world and complain about a lack of leadership in general or values-based leadership in particular. We must be change agents within our organizations, communities, and society at large. The values we embrace must be visible to others by our actions, decisions, and how we interact with and treat others. As I have seen in my own life and career, and in those of many others I have worked with, individuals and organizations can be both financially successful and also a force for good.

One of those examples is Andrew Youn, co-founder of One Acre Fund. After graduating from Kellogg with an MBA, Andrew decided to devote himself and his hard-earned knowledge to addressing the problem of hunger in East Africa. By teaching and promoting best practices in agriculture, One Acre Fund has improved the health and raised the hopes of more than 200,000 farm families, touching more than one million people in Kenya and Rwanda, as well as Burundi and Tanzania. Its goal is to positively impact more than 20 million children by 2025. To salute and support Andrew in his commitment to be his best, I will donate my proceeds from this book (as I do with *From Values to Action*) to One Acre Fund (www.oneacrefund.org).

Guided by self-reflection, informed by a balance of perspectives, and defined by both true self-confidence and genuine humility, values-based leaders at every level make a difference in their organizations. Their values become the basis of their actions and interactions, as they become their best selves. This starts the movement forward in a deliberate process, from best self to best team, best partner, best investment, and best citizen. It is both revolutionary and evolutionary—and it starts with anyone who desires to become a values-based leader.

BEST SELF

A fundamental objective of values-based leadership is answering the question: How do I become my best self?

People at every level and with any job title can and should become values-based leaders—those who lead with principles and live by example. Through their actions, words, and support, values-based leaders utilize the four principles of self-reflection, balance and perspective, true self-confidence, and genuine humility to guide their own actions first. With greater self-awareness and self-knowledge, they bring their *best selves* to work—and motivate and inspire others to do the same.

Leadership is not determined by the number of direct reports or followers you have. You can be a team of one, leading only yourself, and still become a values-based leader by focusing on becoming your best. In fact, for many of us who have reached the C-suite, that's precisely where our values-based leadership began. From your cubicle at the entry level of a company, or working out of your living room as a freelancer, you can put the principles of values-based leadership into action to become your best self, every day.

If you are a middle manager or senior executive, leading a team of 50 or 50,000, grounding your leadership in your *best self* is equally important. It's a dangerous trap to think that having made it to a certain level—even to the C-suite—your focus should look only outward: on developing the organization's goals, achieving targets, and managing others to do their best.

No one is beyond becoming their best self. At this point in my life, I have been CFO, president, CEO, and chairman of a $12 billion global health-care company, with a combined tenure of 11 years at the top of Baxter International. Currently, I'm an executive partner with Madison Dearborn Partners, a Chicago-based private-equity firm, and despite the success I've been lucky to have, I remain just as committed to being my best self as I did when I was starting out in one of those cubicles as a junior analyst, decades ago. As a clinical professor of management and strategy at Northwestern University's Kellogg School of Management, and a frequent speaker for groups of students, new hires, middle managers, and executive leaders, I stress the importance of being your best self as the foundation to values-based leadership.

Your best self is not about perfection (an impossible and, therefore, futile goal). It is about becoming consistently disciplined and focused, making sure you challenge yourself to truly be your best self—instead of becoming complacent, convinced that you have arrived. No matter how good you are, you can always be better. Being your best self is a lifelong commitment.

Becoming your best self will not occur automatically, nor is it a sudden conversion because some emotionally intelligent light switch has been flipped. It is a process, one that will transform you over time and impact every person with whom you come in contact.

Most people have an innate sense of right and wrong and a set of personal values, even if they don't think about them in a concrete way. Most of us strive to be good people, but we're human; we have good days and bad days. There are times when we say things to people that we regret a moment later. We ask ourselves: *Why did I say that? Why did I treat someone like that? Why did I lose my temper with that person? Why did I feel the need to be the know-it-all, instead of valuing others' opinions? Why did I act in ways that are inconsistent with my values?*

The answer is that, in those moments, we were not our best selves. This realization may cause us some embarrassment and discomfort, but the purpose is not to feel shame or beat ourselves up. We simply recommit to the journey of becoming better. Even people whom I greatly admire—spiritual leaders, philanthropists, and executive leaders who truly put others first—admit that they are not their best selves every day. When we acknowledge that we've missed the mark, we're just being honest with ourselves. Then we can recommit to the process of being our best selves, to the best of our ability, every day.

In this section, "Your Best Self," we explore how to use the four principles of values-based leadership to become your best self (which is the foundation for the other *bests* in the book—best team, best partner, best investment, and best citizen). In Chapter 1, we start with the most important principle of values-based leadership: self-reflection. This fundamental principle enhances your self-awareness and self-knowledge, and allows you to gain insight into your decisions, actions, and interactions with others. Self-reflection leads to the second principle of values-based leadership: balance and perspective. I define this second principle as being open to input and diverse opinions from others, and doing so in a way that improves decision-making. From there, in the second chapter, we move to the principles of true self-confidence and genuine humility, which are complementary—not contradictory. With true self-confidence, we ground our best self in the knowledge of our skills and accomplishments; we know what we know. But we also acknowledge what we don't know, and the benefit of working with others who are strong in areas in which we are weak. We reflect on our strengths and weaknesses, and understand what we can become and not become. Genuine humility reminds us of the value of every person, the importance of showing respect to everyone, and never forgetting where we came from.

The four principles of values-based leadership are the road and the guardrails, leading us toward the goal of becoming our best. Like all journeys, it has a clear beginning: becoming your best self.

CHAPTER 1

THE SELF-REFLECTIVE, BALANCED LEADER

S elf-reflection is the most important tool in the values-based leadership toolbox. It is the intentional practice of stepping back, filtering out noise and distractions, and looking inward to gain clarity on what matters most to you, personally and professionally. By being self-reflective, you think deeply about issues so you can make choices that are aligned with your values. You also gain a fuller awareness of the impact of your decisions. Self-reflection also provides you with an opportunity to know yourself better, assess your strengths and weaknesses, and understand where you excel and what areas you need to develop.

Without self-reflection it is impossible to become a values-based leader. Unless you pause to reflect on your priorities and what matters most, you can easily become overwhelmed by the sheer number of items on your to-do list and fail to distinguish between real productivity and pointless activity. Self-reflection can be a potent antidote to the all-too-common experiences of worry, fear, anxiety, pressure, and stress, all of which can undermine your intention to be your best self.

Yet even people who understand the concept of self-reflection struggle with how to put it into practice. In the four years since the publication of my first book, *From Values to Action*, I have given more than 500 talks to diverse audiences, ranging from students to senior leaders in business, government, academia, and the not-for-profit sector, and the dialogue and questions regarding values-based leadership frequently center on the importance of self-reflection. In this chapter, we will start with the foundation of how self-reflection can guide you to become your best self, in every interaction and facing any challenge, every day.

THE IMPORTANCE OF SELF-REFLECTION

Self-reflection is the gateway to self-awareness and self-knowledge. The more you understand yourself, the better you are able to relate to other people. Relating to them allows you to influence them, which is how leadership happens. Values-based leadership moves from the inside out, rooted in the knowledge of what you stand for and what matters most—personally and professionally. All of us lead multifaceted lives, with decisions that impact others, including spouses, partners, and children, as well as colleagues, friends, and team members. The choices we make impact our quality of life.

Self-reflection provides an instant window to what is critically important to you—today, in this moment of your life. You'll make some compromises; everyone does. But you can't really know what you're giving up and the impact of these trade-offs unless you stop to reflect. Otherwise, you will move from activity to activity, from one crisis to another, without a sense of direction or purpose. When you are overwhelmed by everything life is throwing at you, you can't possibly expect to be your best self. That's where self-reflection comes in, helping you prioritize and get back on track.

Often when I talk to people, from students to CEOs, I frequently hear that they are surprised by the consequences of their choices—even things that seem obvious, such as a job requiring extremely long hours or frequent travel. All they know is that they feel out of balance and they aren't living in a way that is consistent with their best selves. The negative aspects of work can quickly become exhausting, even putting a strain on personal relationships and family life. When people suffering from such problems wake up to how stressed and unhappy they are, the source of their trouble often comes as a surprise. The root cause in these situations is typically a lack of self-reflection.

On a business trip to the West Coast, I ran into a former student of mine from Northwestern's Kellogg School of Management at Los Angeles International Airport. When "Joe" reintroduced himself, he reminded me that he had been in my class six years earlier. I remembered him as a very bright individual who had really grasped the principles of values-based leadership as we had discussed them in class. However, when I asked how he was doing, he replied, "Honestly, not very well. I'm really surprised at what's happened in my life."

Joe told me he'd gotten married and had two children, a son and a daughter. Because of his job with an investment bank, which paid him a lot of money, he traveled 90 percent of the time. As a result, he spent very little time with his wife and family, and when he was home, he was exhausted. While Joe was doing very well at the investment bank, and there were aspects of the job he really loved, he wasn't engaged in areas of his life that were important to him, especially his family. In short, he'd lost sight of what he said was crucial to him.

Although I was sympathetic to his situation, I couldn't figure out why he was surprised. It appeared Joe had decided that this professional opportunity and its high salary would be good for him, his career, and his family finances, but he did not self-reflect on the job's broader impact. Self-awareness could have improved his decision-making process, but without it, he was surprised by how stressed and unhappy he had become.

Fortunately, self-reflection is a skill that can be picked up at any time. First, Joe needed to look at things honestly. While he was earning a great salary and bonus, if he analyzed what he was being paid for the actual time he dedicated to his job—accounting for the 80-, 90-, and 100-hour weeks with the pressure of extensive travel and grueling deadlines—he was actually being paid at the rate of a more junior person working a 40-hour week. (When I tell my students this, their faces drop in astonishment, with the realization that *this could happen to me.*)

In our conversation, I never made a recommendation about what Joe should do, or a value judgment about what should be most important to him. He needed to decide that for himself, which he could only do by taking the time (as little as 15 minutes a day of self-reflection) to identify his priorities. If he decided that his career was most important to him at that point in his life, then he needed to be willing to sacrifice time spent on his relationships. That is not a "wrong" or "bad" choice, provided that it is his conscious decision, with a full understanding of the implications. Self-reflection could even help him to identify solutions such as how to spend the little free time he has for the most positive impact and reward.

I asked Joe, "Do you remember how we talked about the importance of self-reflection in class?"

"Of course," Joe replied. "I used to love those assignments, where we had to write a one-page, double-spaced self-reflection every week on our values, goals, and priorities. I guess I got away from doing it."

In the whirl of moving to New York City, being a strong performer (the first guy in the office each morning and the last one to leave at night) and highly regarded at his firm, Joe let self-reflection slip. He stopped asking himself what was most important in his life, what his priorities were, and whether he was comfortable making compromises. Again, I wasn't telling Joe to quit his job at the investment bank, nor do I want to imply that people shouldn't take demanding jobs. I believed that by returning to his habit of self-reflection Joe would find the answers within and would likely seek out someone to be a sounding board. Similarly, each of us is faced with choices, and what we choose should align with becoming our best selves.

SELF-REFLECTION AND THE BUSINESS ORIENTATION OF LEADERSHIP

Students will sometimes say to me, "Harry, for a guy who was a math major, studied accounting, became a CPA, and was a CFO, you sound awfully soft and qualitative with this self-reflection stuff. Where are the hard-core analytics and business results that leadership demands?"

I tell them that self-reflection is based on an analytical approach that results from three equations (or questions) that prove that values-based leadership begins with self-reflection: First, if I am not self-reflective, how can I know myself? Second, if I don't know myself, how can I lead myself? Third, if I can't lead myself, how can I possibly lead other people?

Self-reflection is also valuable as a leadership tool, which I have experienced in my career and have found to be true with other CEOs, who I have the privilege to know. Mark R. Neaman, president and CEO of NorthShore University HealthSystem (see Chapter 6), is a self-reflective leader. One of the ways Mark uses self-reflection is to increase his self-awareness of how he relates to others, so he can exhibit his *best self* as a leader. "When you're a leader, people look to you, trying to anticipate what you'll do or say. Through self-reflection, you increase your awareness of how you are communicating with others. Do you show passion and compassion? Are you hard driving and thinking big thoughts, but never losing your humility because you know you can't accomplish those big dreams all by yourself?" Mark said. "You can't become delusional about how important you are."

Self-reflection as a leadership tool encourages out-of-the-box thinking. Jai Shekhawat is CEO and founder of Fieldglass, which makes the world's most widely used cloud-computing platform for the procurement of contract labor and services. Reflecting on how he picked his first team members (see Chapter 4), Jai chose people with unusual backgrounds to oversee the building and selling of the product. By self-reflecting on what mattered most to him, and therefore to his company, Jai identified his top criteria as passion for the business and capability of delivering what was expected. These two characteristics were more important than having a particular job title or work experience.

Jai obviously had the right team to build the company. Fieldglass was sold in 2014 to SAP of Germany for a reported $1 billion. Even before that market validation, however, Jai knew he'd made good choices for his core team because of the close alignment among the key players, right from the start.

As important as it is to take time by yourself to be self-reflective, it is only half the story. It is equally important to obtain input and feedback from others to make sure you are being realistic and honest with yourself. As my wife, Julie, is fond of telling me, "Harry, left to your own devices, you could convince yourself of anything." No wonder that, after 35 years of marriage, when she asks me if I want her opinion, the answer is always yes. Whether your personal advisor is your spouse or partner, good friend, sibling, mentor, or someone else, make sure you are tapping outside perspectives. The viewpoint of another person can help you see clearly whether something supports your best self or if it's out of sync with who you are and who you say you want to be.

ELIMINATING WORRY, FEAR, ANXIETY, PRESSURE, AND STRESS

There are five words that immediately get everyone's attention in virtually every audience I address: worry, fear, anxiety, pressure, and stress. They are a common experience, and yet most people do not admit to facing them. Self-reflection, though, is the way to shed some light on what you're really feeling, and how to minimize the impact of these negative emotions on your life, so that you can get on with the business of being your best self.

First, you need to acknowledge that worry, fear, anxiety, pressure, and stress are unproductive and unhealthy—just ask your doctor about the impact of stress on your body. Second, through self-reflection you can see that these negative emotions occur most frequently when problems arise, things aren't going well, or when there's a crisis. Suddenly, you're in over your head. Why? Because at some previous point in time, when the first hints surfaced that *maybe this situation, decision, or choice is not going the way I thought it would,* you weren't practicing self-reflection. If you had, you probably would have noticed things going south, or at least you would have been aware of that possibility. Then you could have decided in advance what corrective course of action you'd take when a situation arose or a problem escalated. Even if the situation you find yourself faced with was unforeseeable or beyond your control, self-reflection can ground you in how to respond as *your best self.*

Here's how: Being your best self allows you to live in reality, instead of dwelling in the extremes of believing the good times will last forever, or that difficult episodes will never get better. Self-reflection will keep you on an even keel, by reminding you that no one's life follows the upward slope of a straight line. For all of us, life is a "sine wave" of ups and downs that, we hope, will have an overall upward slope. Self-reflection keeps us grounded in the moment, whether in the midst of highs or lows.

Let's say that life is good right now, personally and professionally. You've got no complaints. That is just fantastic and truly a reason to celebrate—and you should. At the same time, remembering life's sine wave pattern, you know that things are not always going to go well. At some future point in time, there will be a disappointment, upset, or negative event. It's not that you want to douse your happiness today with negativity and worries about tomorrow—by all means enjoy the good times—but being your best self means that you are a realist, preparing yourself *in advance* for when, not if, the downturn happens.

Being self-reflective means that when you're at the top of that sine curve, you already know what you'll do when things don't go so well. You will be alert and prepared for those initial signs of disappointment or upset, and you'll act on them quickly, without getting sidetracked, being surprised, or losing precious energy to worry, fear, anxiety, pressure, or stress. Without self-reflection, you have chosen to wait until a crisis hits to figure out what you're going to do, and by then it's often too late. It's hard to see clearly when you're in the middle of a storm.

With self-reflection I am always prepared to act in the midst of a problem, challenge, or crisis. I will do two things: I will do the right thing, and I will do the best I can. These two seemingly simple, but highly powerful statements have significantly reduced the worry, fear, anxiety, pressure, and stress in my life. No matter what happens—and in senior leadership positions, I have faced my share of crises—I know I will do the right thing and I will do the best I can.

This same thinking allows you, as your best self, to manage the good times and balance the bad times in your organization. Let's say that you're the CEO of a company that has posted strong earnings, quarter after quarter. Perhaps this has occurred for several quarters in a row, and with each successful quarter, the bar gets higher. It's only a matter of time before there is a disappointment, and quarterly earnings, while not bad, are less than investors' expectations. Through self-reflection, you will be prepared for how to respond well in advance of that occurrence: You will do the right thing, and you will do the best you can.

You can plan for anticipated difficulties and the unknown by training yourself to keep things in perspective. Disappointments will occur; that's part of life. The two fundamental commitments— to do the right thing, and to do the best you can—will keep you grounded in reality, no matter what occurs.

While you are being your best self, you may find that some people on your team or other colleagues have a tendency to get worked up in the midst of a problem or crisis—and they may want you to do the same. In fact, if they can't get you all wound up and worried, they think they haven't done their job. During my time at Baxter, after 15 or 20 consecutive quarters of increased earnings, we faced a difficult quarter and, as a result, we were not going to make our projected targets. For example, let's say we had projected quarterly earnings of $1 a share and it looked like we were only going to make $0.90. Such an earnings miss means we would need to tell the Street, and that bad news can cause a lot of worry, fear, anxiety, pressure, and stress. However, by being self-reflective and keeping things in perspective, I remained disciplined and was able to avoid being overwhelmed by negative emotions. One of my colleagues, who got really wound up over the news, said to me, "Harry, don't you realize how serious this is?"

I replied: "Let me see: We will have 550 phone lines to London, Tokyo, and throughout the United States with analysts—buy side and sell side—and large shareholders on a conference call with us, at which time we'll have to give them disappointing news about not making our projections, and that will have a negative impact on our stock price. Am I close?"

Of course I got it, but we didn't have time to waste on being worried and upset. We needed to devote all our time and energy on understanding what happened, why it happened, and what we could do to minimize the chances of it happening again. Being our best selves in that moment meant keeping our commitment to doing the right thing and the best we could do.

CENTERING YOUR BEST SELF

Centeredness is where your best self resides. One of the traps that will throw you out of centeredness is to believe that, when upsets happen, life is *unfair*. The problem is one of perception: Someone believes that life is inherently supposed to be fair. Believe me, I'm no pessimist (in fact, most people who know me would describe me as a strong optimist); my optimism, though, is grounded in realism and the realization I've gained through years of self-reflection that life looks like a normal distribution (i.e., a bell curve). The middle is when things are going okay; to the right are the better-than-normal events (and to the far right the ones that are fantastically wonderful), and to the left are the worse-than-normal events (and to the far left the ones that are tragically so). You, like me, are going to have your share of experiences that fall to the right and left.

Self-reflection and your commitment to being your best self allow you to remain centered, which will increase your resilience in coping with challenging situations and your resourcefulness in finding a solution. You may even be able to minimize the occurrences of some negative events, reducing the incidence of good/bad from the 50/50 of our hypothetical bell curve to 80/20, but I've never met anyone who didn't go through pain and disappointments at least 20 percent of the time.

By being self-reflective, you will be disciplined enough to calmly realize challenges are not exceptions. Failures, deaths, accidents, job losses, and other disappointments are all part of the human experience. Rather than getting mired in the question "*Why did this happen to me?*" you choose to focus on what can be done to make the best of the situation. Interestingly enough, by being proactive, you will be more prepared and less surprised, and better able to reduce the impact of negative events.

BEST SELF IN THE REAL WORLD

Occasionally, someone will say to me, "This sounds great, Harry, but how does it work in the *real world.* I've got a team of people who report to me, and I've got people above me. How can I stay centered as my best self, when I'm caught in the middle of people who are worried, fearful, anxious, pressured, and stressed because of what's happening?"

Even when we're being our best selves and staying centered, we do have to deal with the emotions and reactions of others. Let's take these two groups separately. First, there are the people who report to you (whom we address in more depth in Section Two, "The Best Team"). When an issue or crisis arises, your team members may become flustered and upset because they don't fully understand what's happening, or because they are anxious over what might happen—and so the pressure mounts.

No matter how centered you feel, the anxiety and worry among your team, if left unattended, will escalate into a real problem—even to the point of undermining their ability to respond to the situation. By being your best self and a values-based leader, you can use your own personal example to influence your team. You may need to assure them that they are up to the task in front of them, or remind them of how successfully they've handled problems in the past. As your best self, you will model for others what it means (and looks like) to step back, take a breath, and put the current challenge into perspective. Through your reflective, calm, and thoughtful manner, you will help others adopt a similar demeanor and attitude.

LEADING UP

At this point, you've gotten your personal act together by being your best self, and you've calmed your team by modeling self-reflective behavior for them. But you're still not out of the fire. You still have to deal with *the boss.*

Let's assume that your boss is not self-reflective and does not bring his/her best self to work every day. Instead, this is one of those infamous, out-of-control, the-world-is-coming-to-an-end types of bosses with whom we've all had to deal. This person is not just off-center or lacking self-reflection, but rather a Tasmanian devil! Dealing with this situation requires you to take your best self to another level and *lead up* to manage your boss.

Leading up means using your ability to influence and motivate your boss by your example. You cannot do this without a daily dose of self-reflection on the problems or challenges at hand, the various scenarios and solutions on the table, the personalities involved, your boss's response, and the general state of the atmosphere. As your best self, you are equipped with fine-tuned discernment and emotional intelligence to navigate what will probably be some stormy seas with submerged obstacles!

In my talks, I give a simplified example to show how this can be done. As a strategy is devised and rolled out, your boss says he wants to head east (the hypothetical equivalent of whatever strategic decision is being made at the time). In your opinion, the organization should really be headed west. How you handle this situation, and whether you can influence your boss to reach a better solution, will have an enormous impact on how successful you will be as a leader. It's not just what you do, but how you do it.

Perhaps your boss has a big ego and a tremendous need to be right. Since your commitment, as your best self and a values-based leader, is to do the right thing, you're willing to park your ego at the door. First, you take the time to talk to enough experts to make sure that west really is the optimal direction, and that you're not letting your own ego get in the way. If the consensus is that *west is best*, then you have to present this information in such a way that you influence the boss into reaching the same conclusion—maybe even allowing the boss to think it was his idea. So you might say, "Would it make sense to go west first so that we can do such-and-such?"

Acting as your best self, your objective is not to prove your boss wrong, but to present a better solution. Without having your ego invested in it, your boss can pick up the idea and run with it as if it were his own.

Now, let's say that your boss doesn't want to hear about west. He is convinced that the only way to go is east. Your self-reflection will help you determine whether this really is a big deal, or if it's suboptimal but in the end will probably work out okay. If it's the latter, then you might decide to get on board the boss's eastbound train and figure out how to reach the objectives from there, while doing the right thing and the best you can do.

But let's say that your boss's plan of going east will result in a major problem or setback, and that west really is substantially better (e.g., less risky, significantly more cost-effective or efficient, etc.). If so, it may be time to shoot a so-called *silver bullet*. With self-reflection and being your best self, you will be able to do this because you understand your own motivation. You're not looking for kudos or rewards, to make your boss look foolish or to take his job. You care about the team and the organization, and want the strategy to be successful.

Therefore, with true self-confidence (which we discuss in Chapter 2), in an open and transparent way, you let your boss know that there is a significant difference between going east and going west, and that it makes sense to sit down with the boss the next level up and discuss the situation.

PAUSE FOR REFLECTION

When you are operating as your best self, you have the calmness, centeredness, and clarity to see through the fog. This can only happen if you take the time for daily self-reflection. Personally, I find it best to write down my thoughts in a journal, otherwise it feels too much like just daydreaming. By putting your self-reflection in writing, you also establish a record of your priorities and what you've committed to do.

For me, self-reflection is an activity that's best done at the end of the day, when things calm down from my different jobs and activities (including teaching, speaking, serving on boards of directors, and working in private equity—plus being a husband and father of five). At night, when the children are in bed and I've gotten through my calls and emails, it's time for me to find a quiet place, such as on my back porch or sitting in my favorite chair. For other people, self-reflection is a morning exercise. They center themselves while jogging or walking the dog (jotting down notes on their thoughts afterwards). Others take a 20-minute break during the day and, instead of picking up the phone and calling three more people, they take a walk around the block or the complex. The optimal time and routine will be up to you to discover.

My self-reflection involves a list of questions I ask myself to assess my day and determine whether I've been my best self. For example, did I act in a self-reflective manner, or did I allow myself to get caught up in the emotions and urgency of the day? Did I do what I said I would do, or did I fall short of my own expectations? What did I do well? Where could I have done better? What could I do now to better prepare myself for the next day? How did I treat people? How did I lead people, and how did I follow people? Am I proud of my interactions? Did I keep myself centered, or was I out of control?

As I engage in honest self-reflection, I ask myself what I would do differently if I had the day to live over again. I know I'm a work in progress, and I have the ability to get better. Given what I've learned today, how can I operate better in all dimensions of my life, personally and professionally? The more self-reflective I become, the better equipped I am to be my best self, every day.

BALANCE AND PERSPECTIVE

One of the benefits of becoming self-reflective is gaining balance and greater perspective in your life. As a principle of values-based leadership in action, balance refers to your ability to see a bigger, fuller picture and make decisions accordingly. You don't just rely on what you think or what you know; you purposefully extend your perspective by engaging others. Self-reflection is the tool that allows you to achieve balance most effectively, by allowing you to see when and where you need more input and from which people.

When people are not self-reflective, they also tend to be in a hurry. They're consumed by worry, fear, anxiety, pressure, and stress, and so they think that the only way to counter these negative feelings is by moving quickly. They don't take the time to self-reflect (their first mistake) and they surely don't invest in gathering the input and opinions of others (their second mistake). To them, that would be wasting time, but this viewpoint often leads to a fatal mistake.

When people make quick decisions based on strong opinions and emotions, they usually fail to acknowledge that there are many different perspectives. If understood, other insights could have an enormous impact on anyone's ability to make the best decisions (not just fast ones) and to motivate a team that may have different views on a topic. In my classes and talks, I sometimes encounter immediate negative reactions to this point: "Harry, don't you want me to have a strong opinion and be decisive? Don't you want me to act in an authoritative way as I lead my team? Don't I need to demonstrate that I am, in fact, a decisive leader?" My response is that, in my opinion, it's best to develop strongly held views *after* you have taken the time to truly understand all sides of the issue. (As I tell people, I have *opinions*, not *answers*, and these allow me to keep a balanced perspective.)

I also get pushback from people who say, "I've got a lot to do. I don't have time to hear the opinions of everyone on my team. I have to get an answer to my boss quickly." This argument is based on the narrow perspective that this is a binary choice: Get the team's opinions *or* make a decision quickly. To me, there is no choice involved. As I like to say, if the question is whether to seek the opinions of people who can add value *or* to make a decision quickly, the answer is *yes*.

At every level of the organization, being your best self means you value balance and perspective in your decision making (which we will revisit in the dynamic of a *best team*). That doesn't mean you will drag out the process, engage in *paralysis by analysis*, or procrastinate by chasing after the trivial and tangential. If the decision you have to make can be better, stronger, or more assured by reaching out to a colleague or team member whose input you can gather quickly, then being your best self demands that you do both.

Another aspect of balance is to recognize that you don't have all the answers. No matter how much experience you have or how high up you are in the organization, there are others (and often they are junior people) who have valuable perspectives and experiences. One example is social media, which many organizations are still trying to get a handle on pairing with their traditional marketing and communications strategies. If you're the chief marketing officer, you may be a best-in-class expert in the traditional channels, but when it comes to employing social media, the person with more knowledge may be a 20-something. When it comes to very fast-moving technology, someone with only one to two years in the organization may actually be more knowledgeable than a more senior person. (Personally, I am the first to admit that my 12-year-old son, Daniel, is far more adept at electronics than I am, and if it weren't for him, my DVD player would blink 12:00.)

Being your best self means you acknowledge the critical importance of gathering diverse opinions and viewpoints from people of different ages, backgrounds, ethnicities, cultures, and genders. Furthermore, being your best self as a values-based leader means you are committed to motivating and elevating your team. Balance and perspective also enable you and your team to gain a broader understanding that enhances your contribution—or, as I like to say, you can see the trees and the forest, rather than getting caught up in the root system!

A BALANCED INDIVIDUAL

When you act with balance, others will perceive you to be a balanced individual—a true sign of someone being his or her best self. Consider the example of one executive vice president at a company where I was asked to give a presentation. As we discussed the importance of balance in all aspects of life, this executive, whom we'll call Mary Ellen, said that she believed that exercise was key to her health and was something she definitely needed to do. "I am trying to exercise more," she said, "but I just don't have the time to do it."

I asked Mary Ellen if she put exercise on her calendar with the same regularity and commitment as her nine o'clock meeting and her noon client lunch. "If it's not on your calendar," I told her, "you won't do it. You'll tell yourself that you'll wait until everything else is done. But guess what? You'll never get everything else done."

At this point, Mary Ellen's colleague, we'll call him Ron, piped up that he had a similar problem. Ron's job required him to travel extensively and very often the fitness centers at his hotels closed at nine in the evening. I explained that I travel about 50 percent of the time, and very often I don't get to my hotel until after ten o'clock at night, which is why I try to avoid staying in hotels that don't have 24-hour fitness centers.

The point to this story is simple: If you say something is important to you—if it is key to balance and being your best self—then you have to make it a priority. Otherwise, you will not come across as disciplined, focused, consistent, and credible—to yourself or others. Saying you *don't have the time* for something really means it's not a high enough priority for you to *make* time. (As I discuss in *From Values to Action*, we all have 168 hours per week. The only question is how we spend that time.) With self-reflection and balance, you can make choices for yourself that enable you to become your best self in everything you do.

SELF-REFLECTION AND BALANCE— COMPLEMENTARY TOOLS IN THE LEADERSHIP TOOLBOX

Your pursuit of balance and perspective is accomplished most effectively through self-reflection. How else are you going to see what you need and whom you need to engage? As you reflect on what is being asked of you—the options you are weighing, the decisions you need to make—you will identify those experts who can provide valuable perspective and input.

This is a powerful benefit of self-reflection. While self-reflection remains highly important for heightening your self-awareness, providing you with feedback on your actions, and letting you know whether you are being your best self, this foundational principle is really an all-purpose tool. Self-reflection isn't limited to talking to yourself like a hermit in a cave. Inner dialogue, while meaningful, is not the only dimension of self-reflection.

Being your best self means you utilize self-reflection to enhance your engagement in community with others, which improves your balance and broadens your perspective. Purposefully seeking out feedback from others keeps you grounded in reality instead of slipping into a kind of dream world of unexamined perception.

YOUR BEST SELF, EVERY DAY

At every level, leadership starts with you. While living and working in the real world puts you in contact with others, you cannot move too quickly into the communal and organizational before you've done sufficient work on the personal. At a fundamental level, your best self—the core of the concentric circles of *bests* that radiate from you through the organization and into society—determines what you stand for, what matters most, how you will act, and how you will treat others. People need to take the time to define what best self means to them. Once they have a clear picture, they can self-reflect each day to determine if they lived and demonstrated it. Becoming one's best self starts with self-reflection. By being honest with yourself, you will know how well you are keeping your word, honoring your values, and living in accordance with your priorities. You will limit or even eliminate unpleasant surprises, and carry out your twin commitments of doing the right thing and doing the best you can do. Self-reflection will help you achieve balance and a broader perspective. Others will perceive you as being focused, disciplined, consistent, and credible in everything you undertake, professionally and personally. In short, you will be well on your way to being your best self, every day.

CHAPTER 2

THE HUMBLE, SELF-CONFIDENT LEADER

I t sounds like a contradiction or maybe even an oxymoron: a humble, self-confident leader. How can someone be both humble and self-confident? The truth is, as you continue your journey of becoming your best self, in addition to self-reflection and balance, there are two more essential tools in the values-based leadership toolbox: true self-confidence and genuine humility.

These two principles of values-based leadership are discreet, standalone traits; one is not contingent upon the other like some kind of balancing act. To be your best self, you need more true self-confidence *and* more genuine humility at every level, whether you are beginning your career, a new manager with a small team to lead, or a senior executive in charge of a large division, region, or an entire company. True self-confidence and genuine humility are the distinguishing characteristics that will showcase your values and highlight your authenticity.

TRUE SELF-CONFIDENCE: WHAT I KNOW AND WHAT I DON'T KNOW

Confidence is one of those words that people think they understand. They equate it with being sure of yourself, knowing what you're doing, or being decisive. They might describe it in terms of a physical appearance or presence: head up and shoulders back with good posture. But what does it really mean to be confident—or, using our terminology here, to have true self-confidence? Clearly, it can be an elusive quality that is hard to define.

The *Wall Street Journal*'s June 2014 *WSJ. Magazine* asked "six luminaries" (their description, not mine) to describe confidence. A tennis player notes that, "The guys with the most success tend to have the most confidence." A supermodel, who relates how she fell off high platform shoes on a runway, says, "If you carry yourself like you have confidence, you could actually have it or you could not, but we'll never know, will we?" A high-wire artist says he could not answer "the mysterious question" of where he found the confidence to undertake his aerial feats.[1] And on it goes . . .

While such insights might make for entertaining reading, I don't find them very helpful. If confidence is only appearing or acting in a certain way, how is that authentic? If you need success to have confidence, then how do you get the confidence to become successful? Further, if confidence is a mysterious, indescribable quality how can you develop it to become your best self?

Wherever you are in life, true self-confidence comes from the knowledge of who you are and what you stand for, which you define (and redefine) every day through self-reflection. You acknowledge your skills and accomplishments; you don't need to pretend to be anything more than what you are (this is *true* self-confidence). There is no posturing or pretending that you are the one with all the answers, the person who can do anything. No matter

---

[1] The Columnists, *WSJ. Magazine,* June 2014.

how good you are at something, true self-confidence is never about being arrogant, egotistical, and obnoxious. You know that there will always be others who are more intelligent, articulate, athletic, successful, and so on than you are, but you are okay with that. Equally important, you know what you don't know and you willingly admit it to others. You embrace your strengths and weaknesses.

True self-confidence comes down to a simple statement: *I know what I know, and I know what I don't know.* Let's take them one at a time.

You may be someone who has natural gifts; perhaps you're very good at mathematics or mechanics, writing or music. Alternatively, you may be someone who, although not endowed with an incredible amount of natural talent, has quickly come up the learning curve through a combination of drive, discipline, studiousness. Maybe you struggle to gain expertise and competency in certain areas, but through perseverance, a strong work ethic, and a lot of effort, you develop a specific skill set or knowledge base. Wherever you fall along the talent and competency continuum, you know what you know. You take pride in your accomplishments and what you've attained.

That's not to say that you've arrived at the top; you are not being complacent. As a disciplined person, you know you can always get better, but you do have true self-confidence in your achievements. Through self-reflection you appreciate that the glass is half full. You have opportunities to learn much more, but you don't get consumed by all the things you don't know. That empty half of the glass is waiting to be filled with future growth, as you make progress toward becoming your best self and a values-based leader. This is an adaptive process that you can practice over a lifetime.

TRUE AND FALSE SELF-CONFIDENCE

When I make presentations, a common reaction from my students at Northwestern's Kellogg School of Management, as well as executives, is to ask why I describe this principle as *true* self-confidence. As they see it, it stands to reason that someone is either self-confident or they're not. There are people, however, (and many of us have worked for and with them) who can act very self-confident, but in reality, they have no self-confidence. They try to make others believe their illusion so that their lack of substance, shortfall of skills, and low self-confidence won't show. I call this the *macho group*, who insist that others should "do what I tell them to do, because I never make a mistake."

A person with *false* self-confidence likes and even needs to be put on a pedestal, so that others think, *Wow, she's so amazing; she is never wrong*, or, *That guy is a superstar—there is nobody quite like him*. Leadership, however, is not a prize earned by having the most accomplishments or the most impressive titles and positions. As a values-based leader fully committed to being your best self, you know that leadership requires followership. Others will only follow you if you can relate to them, and they to you.

On the other hand, if you have difficulty embracing what you know and what you have accomplished, self-reflection is a valuable tool. In your daily quiet time, you can ask yourself why you have trouble acknowledging your skills, talents, and achievements. Are you intimidated by others who appear to be more successful or talented? Do you think that others don't recognize you, or that they will put you down for your ideas? In meetings and presentations, do you feel unprepared? Are you nervous that someone will ask you a question that you can't answer? (We'll discuss the solution later in the chapter.) Self-reflection will help you get to the root causes of why you lack true self-confidence, and how you can *know what you know* over time.

As a mathematics and economics major, I have always been confident of the fact that, if anyone describes anything to me regarding economics or finance, once I hear the concept I can grasp it automatically; it comes very naturally to me. However, if something is mechanical in nature, even after hearing it described three or four times, I still won't understand it. I joke that if someone asks me what kind of heat I have in my house, the only answer I can give is "hot heat." I think a toilet that flushes is a miracle. Knowing what I *don't know*, I keep the phone numbers of good HVAC contractors and plumbers handy.

You know what you know, and what you don't know. This is the balanced perspective that comes with true self-confidence. In order to have fuller understanding and deeper knowledge, you need to surround yourself with people who know more than you do about certain things. For some people, especially those who have accomplished a lot in their lives, the *what-you-don't-know* part is a considerable challenge.

THE TWO-QUESTION TEST

After one of my presentations at a large company, "Jeffrey," a senior vice president, asked how people could determine whether they have true self-confidence. I told him that true self-confidence was revealed by asking two questions. The first is: Have you reached a point in your life where you are willing to say, "I don't know?" The second is: Can you admit to having made a mistake?

Jeffrey listened politely, but I could tell he was struggling with both concepts, especially the first of admitting what he didn't know. As he saw it, knowing what you know and what you don't know might be fine for a junior person, but as a senior vice president, he was the go-to person for information and insight in his division. How could he tell the CEO "I don't know?" He thought it was better to give a half answer or a *guesstimate* than no answer at all.

Beyond the absurdity that someone could possibly know *everything*, there is another point to be made here: You have to become comfortable with what you don't know. It takes true self-confidence to readily admit—whether to a boss, to peers, or to direct reports— that you don't have the answer (but you do, in fact, know where to get it). A senior leader who is able to admit that would be refreshing for most people. And by the way, the teammates won't be a bit surprised to learn that the boss isn't a font of all knowledge.

That was news to "Maria," a senior executive at another company, who, like Jeffrey, said she was not comfortable letting her team know what she didn't know. Maria had more than 500 people working for her, and couldn't see any advantage in admitting any shortfall in her knowledge or understanding. "I'm the kind of person who holds her cards close to the vest, so I would rather not admit what I don't know," Maria said.

I had to break the news to Maria: *Her colleagues already knew what she didn't know,* especially her direct reports. Maria was absolutely shocked. "How can they not know?" I asked her. "They work closely with you every day."

In my presentations when I discuss, "What the boss doesn't know," I'm always greeted with wide smiles and lots of nodding. I tell my audience, "Don't raise your hand in case your boss is in the room. Couldn't you write a book about all the things your current or previous boss doesn't know or isn't good at?" Everyone, including most bosses in the room, always laughs at that one!

I don't mean to imply that all bosses are incompetent. It's just a fact of life that no one knows everything. Therefore, a boss who can admit what he or she doesn't know is more likely to inspire loyalty among the team than someone who, like Maria, keeps those knowledge cards close to the vest. As I used to say back in the early days of my career, I always hoped there were things that my boss didn't know, because if my boss knew everything there would be no reason to keep me around, and with five children I needed a job.

When it comes to self-confidence, junior people also struggle with admitting what they don't know, usually out of fear (read: they lack true self-confidence) of what their bosses will think. Will they be perceived as not having done their homework, or not knowing as much as someone else on the team (who is probably just posturing)? As I tell my Kellogg students, when your boss asks you a question that you can't immediately answer, it is perfectly acceptable to reply, "How fast do you need that answer? Rather than guess, I'm going to find someone who really knows."

That response won't make you appear to be asleep at the switch, or undisciplined about learning. Rather, you'll show that you have the integrity and true self-confidence not to waste the boss's time with a non-answer.

At the same time, there is no virtue in beating yourself up for what you don't know (and this certainly isn't genuine humility, as we'll discuss in a moment). If all you do is focus on what you don't know and the skills that you lack, others will perceive you as totally lacking confidence. By owning what you do know, you allow others to see your potential and how much more you can learn.

Similarly, when a project or assignment is completed, you can acknowledge what went right and what went wrong, while still feeling good about yourself. Your self-reflection might go something like this: *Yes, I could have done better and I could have done more. But my team and I actually did a good job. I'm going to reflect positively on what went well, congratulate the team on what we accomplished, and be conscious of what we can do better so that we can focus our efforts there the next time.* No matter what the project or activity, almost by definition some things will go well and some things will not. Everything (including ourselves) is a work in progress.

ADMITTING WHEN YOU'RE WRONG

As I explained to Jeffrey, the senior vice president, there is a second question to determine whether someone has true self-confidence: Can you admit to being wrong? Here's where many people stumble over their egos, fears of being seen as foolish or inexperienced, and their own stubbornness.

The truth is, sometimes you will be right and sometimes you will be wrong. Instead of being caught up in the impossible predicament of always needing to be right, it's far better to admit your fallibility. When a decision you made turns out to be wrong, you quickly admit it to your team. By doing so, you empower everyone to find what will work, whether to amend the plan, change direction, or take other corrective steps. People who need to be right all the time create turmoil for everyone around them, because they can't admit to having made a mistake until it becomes obvious—or until they find some circumstance or person to blame for why their brilliant idea fell short.

Worse yet are those who never make a decision so they can never be wrong. Instead, they just talk and talk, expounding upon various ideas and options, while never giving their team direction. As I related in my first book, I can remember being a young analyst listening to a boss talk about a product launch, and afterwards scratching my head over what he told us to do. Sitting in my cubicle I debated with a colleague over whether the decision was to go ahead or not; one of us thought yes and the other thought no.

Being young and inexperienced, we blamed ourselves for not listening as well as we should have. If we had been more experienced and probably a little cynical, we might have said the boss didn't describe things very well. The truth was that the boss was one of those individuals with a talent for talking a lot without really saying anything. He never made a decision, so he was never wrong! It's a curious skill set (some politicians are pretty good at this), but it almost always ends in chaos. Under such ambiguous conditions, the only way anything gets done is for someone to have the true self-confidence to make a decision.

TRUE SELF-CONFIDENCE AND LEADERSHIP

When I am interviewing someone, I look for signs of true self-confidence. It's relatively straightforward to determine. A person who is truly self-confident can discuss her accomplishments, while at the same time give credit to her team. Rather than everything being all about herself, the candidate is comfortable acknowledging the contributions of others. In addition, when asked about something that didn't work out, she has no problem describing failures and what she learned from them.

With true self-confidence, you can view every experience, good or bad, as a learning experience. In everything, you can find an opportunity to be stretched and challenged, acquire new skills, and learn about yourself. In the process, you will advance toward becoming your best self.

In my role as an executive partner for Madison Dearborn Partners, a private equity firm, I talk with leaders of various companies and advise the executives of the firms in our portfolio. (I sit on the boards of four of these firms, and I am the board chairman of one.) What a difference there is between leaders who use "I" in every sentence and those who say "we" and mean it. Charismatic leaders sometimes create organizations that are overly dependent on them, a scenario that often ends in failure. Certainly, strong leadership at the top of an organization is an asset, but I've never seen a company that ran on the strength of one individual. The key to a company's success is the team. Leaders with true self-confidence readily acknowledge that fundamental truth.

Similarly, your true self-confidence will attract people who want to work with and for you, whether you're a team member or a team leader. As counterintuitive as it may seem, admitting what you don't know and acknowledging your mistakes actually leads to more success, whether at the entry level, in a middle-management position, or even as a CEO. Not only will people experience your best self, they also will have a better chance of relating to you and wanting to be part of the network of contacts and experts you turn to for the information and answers that you need.

At this point, you have gained insights into the first three principles of values-based leadership—self-reflection, balance and perspective, and true self-confidence—and how they support you in becoming your best self. Now, we move on to the fourth principle of values-based leadership: genuine humility.

GENUINE HUMILITY

Genuine humility reminds you that everyone deserves respect; no one is more important than anyone else. As a values-based leader, genuine humility allows you to acknowledge the contributions of your team and to put the spotlight on them, not only in your team meetings, but also in front of *your* boss. With the power of self-reflection, genuine humility lets you see how and where you can extend a helping hand to others. You don't allow yourself to become too busy to do something for someone else.

As motivating and inspiring as that sounds, this is the principle most likely to get an eye roll. When I'm addressing a group of middle managers and executives, genuine humility sometimes comes across as being "nice" or "cute." They rarely recognize it as a sign of strong leadership. No matter; when I see those blank stares in my audience, I get to work.

Here's what I tell them: Leadership is all about the ability to influence. (Heads nod in agreement.) You can't influence people if you can't relate to them. (More heads nod.) How can you relate to anyone if you have forgotten what it was like to be in their position? (Now I've got their attention.)

Ask yourself: Do you remember what it was like when you first started out in your career? Have you forgotten how it felt to be the new person, the one who didn't know who to go to with questions, who felt intimated by the bosses? Do you still remember life in *the cube?*

Starting out as a junior analyst, I, like all my cubicle-mates, observed the bosses. *Those guys* (a gender-neutral term) always seemed to be rushing around from one meeting to another. They never had time for us, except when they needed data, in which case we had to come up with it—fast! *Those guys* made all the decisions, which sometimes seemed pretty illogical to those of us in "the cubes," even though we were on the frontlines implementing them. We could tell which plans were going to work, which ones would not, and which ones the customers would hate—and we were often right. But *those guys* usually did not go to the cubes for input; they made the decisions and we tried our best to put them in action.

Back in those days, being a senior leader like *those guys* felt far beyond my reach, but I told myself that if I ever became a team leader or a manager, I would never forget the cube.

I always ask my audience of executives and senior leaders to think back on those early days in their careers, and the few people who made them feel comfortable and showed them the ropes. As I remind them, these were the people who took the time to reach out directly, to stop by the cubicles to talk to junior people and invite them to lunch. They made you feel like part of the organization. Back then, you might have said to yourself, "When I'm a boss or a manager one day, or even a vice president, I'm going to act like this person who has been so helpful to me. I'm going to be the one who sits in the cafeteria with the new team members or who stops by a cubicle to see how things are going."

But how many of you, 10, 20, or 30 years later, have to admit that you didn't live up to that promise because you tell yourself you don't have the time? The way you see it, they'll figure it out (or not), they'll grow up and catch on, even though that wasn't your experience when you were starting out. You *did* have someone help you. Others went out of their way to support you. Being where you are today and with all you've accomplished, somehow you've forgotten one of the most important things— something you vowed you'd never lose sight of: You forgot where you came from.

After one such talk, an executive vice president came over to me during a break. He was misty-eyed as he admitted, "Clearly, I have not taken the time to remember where I came from, and that was something that, long ago, I promised myself I would never do. Going forward, I'm going to embrace this concept of *remembering the cube.*"

THE GENUINELY HUMBLE LEADER

Rick Waddell, chairman and CEO of Northern Trust, is an impressive leader. Intelligent, articulate, and with strong values, he led his company through the turbulence of the financial crisis with strong leadership and the highest professional standards (as we discuss in Chapter 8). To me, Northern Trust is an exemplary company that truly exhibits its mission and values, and Rick personifies those qualities.

At the same time, Rick embodies the genuinely humble leader. He describes a "paradigm-shifting moment" in 1987,[2] when Northern Trust's then-CEO Wes Christopherson asked Rick, who was managing one of the bank's lending divisions, to be his strategic planning officer. When Rick met with Wes for the first time to learn about the expectations of the job, he was given an assignment: draw an organizational chart of Northern Trust.

As he sat in the CEO's office, Rick started drawing the chart from the top, with a small circle marked "CEO." Below that, he wrote down the two or three people who reported directly to Wes, and then another level of more people, and still more people on the level below that, so that the org chart resembled a pyramid. "Stop," Wes told Rick after a few minutes. Taking the chart, Wes turned it upside down. In the blank space at what was now the top of the chart, Wes wrote "clients." Below that, he marked down the "real leaders" of the organization—the bankers, portfolio managers, operations staff, and others with the closest client contact. "These folks are the true leaders of the organization," Wes told Rick.

At the bottom of the inverted org chart, was the CEO—representing, as Wes described, that his job was to work for everyone else, supporting them in any way he could. "I work for you,"

---

[2] Rick Wadell, telephone interview, September 3, 2014. Quotes and data regarding Northern Trust Corporation come from this interview unless footnotes indicate otherwise.

Wes told Rick. "When you figure out what you need me to do to help you do your job, let me know."

That "five-minute conversation," as Rick recalls, demonstrated the importance of leaders being visible and available to support others. Now, as CEO, Rick regularly goes to the cafeteria where he sits down with different groups of people and joins the conversation to listen and learn. He has positioned his desk so that anyone passing by his office can see him through his door that is always open. His assistant knows that any time someone wants to talk to him, he is available.

This isn't for show or to make others think that he's a great guy (which he is). Rather, Rick sees these attitudes and behaviors as fundamental to him being his best self every day as the chairman and CEO of Northern Trust. As Rick's example shows, genuine humility reminds you that every person in the organization is valued and makes a contribution, and that everybody on the team can come up with great ideas. People who actually do much of the work—team members on the production line, or in client service call centers— often have the best insights into day-to-day operations, client satisfaction, and even changes in the marketplace.

Genuine humility diminishes the "I" and elevates the "we," and not in a false way, like the boss who notices the team members once or twice a year, with a blanket "thanks for all you do"—not that he or she has any idea who is doing what two levels below. Genuine humility reminds us that we're all in this together.

HOW DID YOU GET TO WHERE YOU ARE?

The challenge for some people is that they don't remember the cube and they forget where they came from. In the leadership talks I give around the world to individuals at many levels of their organizations, I ask participants two questions: "How did you get to where you are today? To what do you attribute your success?" I almost always get the same responses: *I work very hard* and *I have certain skill sets.*

Hard work and having valuable skills are very important to anyone's success, including mine, but through self-reflection and taking the time to really know myself, I also see that four other factors influenced my success. The first is luck. Yes, you have to be prepared for opportunities when they arise and, to a certain extent, you do make your own luck. But luck is definitely a factor. Second, and closely related to luck, is timing—being in the right place at the right time.

The third factor is having a great team, including all of the people with whom I've had the good fortune to work, who took the time to help me early on. If it weren't for the quality of the people on those teams and their dedicated efforts to accomplish our goals and objectives, I would not have achieved what I have in my career. The fourth is more personal and reflective: having a spiritual perspective; that is, I see my talents and the opportunities I've had as gifts that were given to me.

With this perspective, I know I'm not the only party to my success. An enormous part is due to fortuitous circumstances I cannot take credit for and the countless people who helped me along the way and contributed to my achievements. This realization is very humbling, but genuinely so. It does not rob me of any satisfaction. Rather, it gives me deeper appreciation for the journey thus far and the people who have made it enjoyable, engaging, challenging, and rewarding. I look beyond myself and see so many others, a perspective that is invaluable to being my best self.

As a values-based leader, you recognize that beyond hard work and skill sets are luck, timing, the team, and a reflective and spiritual perspective that all play a part in your success. Therefore, you must keep things in context, remember where you came from, and never read your own press clippings (but if you read them, don't believe them). Finally, make sure you keep your genuine humility by surrounding yourself with people (family members, friends, colleagues) who knew you *way back when* and won't allow you to get caught up in yourself.

CAN YOU *REALLY* BE TRULY SELF-CONFIDENT AND GENUINELY HUMBLE IN THE REAL WORLD?

With true self-confidence, you know what you know, and what you don't know. Genuine humility reminds you where you came from and the importance of every person. But how do these principles work in the real world? It's a question I'm often asked by students and executives. Not only are they reluctant to admit what they don't know, they are also concerned that by being humble, others will take advantage of them. As they observe in their organizations, the people who get ahead are often the squeaky wheels who demand the bosses' attention; they are vocal about their needs and aren't shy about taking credit for accomplishments.

One mid-level executive told me, "If I don't take the credit for what I do, I'm afraid it will go unacknowledged, and then I won't be given the opportunities to take on bigger responsibilities that will lead to promotions and better assignments so I can advance my career." This executive appeared absolutely sincere when he told me, "Harry, what I think I need is *less* genuine humility and *more* true self-confidence."

Contrary to what people might believe, these two principles of values-based leadership are not contradictory, nor are they a balancing act. Both are essential to becoming your best self. I explained to this executive that true self-confidence and genuine humility are not stuck on a sliding scale, where adding self-confidence reduces humility and vice versa. In fact, there is never a time when you want less of one and more of another. You always want more of both.

No matter how much true self-confidence you have, you can still use more. And, regardless of how genuinely humble you are, you can still be more so. It goes back to being your best self and the concept of values-based leadership. As your best self, you fully appreciate that, every day, you can gain more true self-confidence to acknowledge who you are, what you know, and what you do not know. Your genuine humility makes others feel like they really do belong to a team. You value them for their contributions, especially in areas where they have strengths that you do not have. Your teammates are not cogs in a wheel, but co-contributors to the greater whole.

By employing the four principles of values-based leadership—self-reflection, balance, true self-confidence, and genuine humility—you become your best self as part of your journey to become a values-based leader. Now, you are ready to move to the next ring in our concentric circle, as your best self becomes the bridge to building the best team.

BEST TEAM

On a best team, every person knows that what he or she does truly matters, and commits to doing—and being—their best.

The journey that begins with your best self now continues as you join together with other values-based individuals to form a best team. Each team member, acting as his or her best self, understands what the team is trying to accomplish, and how each person contributes to achieving the goals and objectives of the values-based organization.

All too often, however, when teams form, the people involved have little or no understanding of how their particular function contributes to an organization's larger mission. They assume it must all come together somewhere and somehow, but they cannot link what they do with the greater whole. When this happens, it's impossible to have a best team because there is no clear, elevating goal to create alignment.

A best team is formed when people are self-reflective, understand themselves, and come together with a sense of common purpose. It takes each person operating as his or her best self for the group to function extremely well together. As their best selves, team members are self-reflective, balanced, have true self-confidence, and are

49

genuinely humble. They know that it is not about them; they speak about "we," not "I."

In order to more fully understand what a best team is, let's be clear about what it is not. A best team is not a collection of superstars who, like some highly paid professional athletes, focus on their own glory, stats, and individual achievements. When some billionaire tries to bring together star athletes who don't work together, the result is rarely a best team and usually a very expensive failure. It is much better to find people who are not individual stars, but who have the capability and desire to work well together, such that the collective activity of the team is greater than each individual contribution.

Among younger professional colleagues there can be some jealousy or competition. Two interns, for example, may—consciously or unconsciously—feel that they have to compete with each other in order to succeed. They may even be intimidated by each other (not being truly self-confident in their own credentials) and feel compelled to demonstrate their higher worth compared to the other. Some organizations encourage such competition, believing it will incentivize better performance. This is certainly not how a best team operates. On a best team, instead of competing with each other, everyone works to bring out the best in themselves and others.

Another characteristic of a best team is that members are free and empowered to challenge each other openly and strongly—not to offend someone, but to enhance the contribution of every individual and of the entire team. When one best-team member questions another, it's clear that the only motivation is to bring out the best in the team. This runs contrary to what a lot of people believe. They erroneously assume that, to be a great team, people have to play nice with each other. They think that challenging each other and questioning the merits of a particular decision or proposal means that the people on the team don't like or respect one another. To them, that's not how best teams interact. They expect that people will agree without questioning each other.

On best teams, everyone's input is valued, even if it runs counter to general sentiment. There is no giving in to someone who feels the need to have his way most of the time. Nor will a best team tolerate someone who is not being her best self because she is more concerned with being right than discovering the right thing to do. Teams that devolve into those ways of thinking will never be best.

A critical component of the best team is a strong values-based team leader, who strives to be respected rather than liked. The leader understands the critical importance of feedback, and that giving open, honest, continuous, and transparent feedback is not simply a good thing to do; it is a moral responsibility to the best team and each of its members. People can only realize their potential when they understand their strengths as well as their weaknesses.

One of the challenges that leaders face trying to pull together a best team is that, while individual members may be hard-working and well-intentioned, they can focus too narrowly on their own activity. Because they cannot see how their particular tasks, role, department, or division relates to the greater whole of the organization, they tend to stay in their silo. As I relate in my talks to students and executives, these are the individuals who, while bright and competent, don't see the forest because they get lost in the trees. They may have seen one or two trees, but they have no sense that there's a forest involved at all!

The values-based leader makes sure that every person sees the forest and understands his or her relationship to the clear, elevating goals of the organization. They know that by expanding each person's view, by broadening horizons and instilling a sense of purpose, that they are able to create an effective best team. These are the teams that can effectively function from the roots to the trees to the forest.

During group interaction, leaders who operate as their best selves don't need to be the first to talk. Instead these leaders almost always hold their opinions until everyone else has spoken, so they don't suppress true discussion. This makes these leaders excellent communicators, since they spend 90 percent of their time listening. Additionally, team members appreciate these leaders' balance and perspective as well as the time they spend understanding all sides of an issue.

A values-based leader of a best team realizes the critical importance of being able to relate uniquely to each member, which is crucial to motivating others since each person is influenced by different things. For some, motivation is largely monetary; others thrive on individual recognition. Some appreciate having flexible work hours in order to accommodate their personal needs, such as childcare or taking care of an elderly parent. Leaders who know how to relate to and motivate each person individually, can bring teams together more effectively.

In the next two chapters, we will look at creating a best team in two distinct environments. In Chapter 3, we find ourselves in a large corporation that, for a variety of reasons, has become dysfunctional and plagued by infighting. Employee engagement is at a low rate, which causes good people to leave the company. The only hope is for a strong, values-based leader to stage a turnaround and forge a best team that extends across the company, with people who are able to collaborate, cooperate, and challenge each other to their highest levels of creativity and productivity. Over time and with concerted effort, a best team emerges out of what had been poorly functioning and unmotivated groups of individuals. Featured in this discussion is Douglas Conant who served as president and CEO of Campbell Soup Company, from 2001 to 2011. When it comes to real-world experience in turning around a team, starting with its values, one of the best examples is what Doug accomplished at Campbell.

In Chapter 4 we explore how the best-team concept is incorporated into a start-up, a lean organization that does not have a lot of resources and needs people to perform multiple roles. In this environment, a company needs to have a best team for two important phases: the launch of the company and as it scales up in size.

We will hear from Jai Shekhawat, founder of human-capital technology company Fieldglass, who has joined the ranks of highly successful entrepreneurs whose great ideas not only scaled from concept to company, but also attracted the attention of a much bigger organization. As Jai demonstrates, the values-based entrepreneurial leader looks for team members with the right skill set and complementary backgrounds, who can generate out-of-the-box thinking, while still creating alignment and cooperation.

While many organizations give lip service to the concept of teamwork and to the adage that *people are our most important asset*, creating and sustaining a best team takes far more than slogans and platitudes. A values-based enterprise that pursues aggressive goals, while also serving a greater purpose, fosters best teams across the company, in every division and function, and at every level in the organization. The best team is the building block for current and future success.

CHAPTER 3

TURNING AROUND A TEAM

At the height of the dysfunction, when all the arrows are pointing downward and problems are not only apparent, they are sometimes front-page news, people begin to wonder: *What went wrong?* Sometimes the problems are evident long before they wreak havoc. While founders or leaders may have had innovative ideas and unique products, the culture can change to one that is no longer values-based. Without a strong foundation of values-based principles, it's very hard to create a sustainable organization. In fact, a lack of values contributes to company failures the vast majority of the time.

Often, though, organizations do start off right. Over the course of their history, they achieve great success. These companies become household names, well recognized by customers and consumers. At least in the beginning, the right people are in place, many of whom are committed to being their best selves. They develop best teams that are highly productive. They have strong partnerships and generate an attractive shareholder return. But something happens. The environment becomes toxic and then everything falls apart.

What had been a best team dissolves into a dysfunctional group, rife with infighting, conflict, and chaos. As things go from bad to worse, people wonder: How did this happen? As we will read in this chapter with the example of the Campbell Soup Company, even well-known, iconic companies can fall into this trap.

FROM BEST TO BROKEN: WHAT CAN GO WRONG

There are many scenarios that can bring an organization to brokenness. One occurs during the expansion phase. For example, when a company was launched, the initial team was composed of people who lived by their values. They were their best selves and motivated to make a difference to their customers and clients. But over time, as the company grew, leaders did not create clear expectations around values that people were expected to follow, so new people who were recruited to the company were often inconsistent with the organization's founding values. Furthermore, as these individuals, who were not acting as their best selves were promoted into leadership positions, they were unequipped to create best teams. It doesn't take many bad apples to spoil the entire barrel. A lack of values among even a few people, whose negative influence spreads, can destroy the entire organization.

Culture shifts can happen gradually as a result of increasingly bad morale, or they can be swift, with a sudden change in leadership or management focus. Along the way, what once made a company great can be lost. One example of an iconic American institution that went from great to broken is Motorola. From its founding in 1928, Motorola distinguished itself with a history that included "the first car radios, the first handheld mobile phones, the first device to carry voice and video from the moon to the earth."[1]

---

[1] Ted C. Fishman, "What Happened to Motorola," *Chicago Magazine*, September 2014. www.chicagomag.com/Chicago-Magazine/September-2014/What-Happened-to-Motorola/.

With a strong culture of innovation, Motorola enjoyed a trajectory of growth that took it to a market capitalization of more than $53 billion by 2006. Since then, Motorola, now known as Motorola Solutions (after spinning off Motorola Mobility), has lost 75 percent of its combined market capitalization.

What brought about Motorola's fall? The company brought in CEOs from the outside, which led to a loss of entrepreneurial spirit, as the focus shifted from balancing short- and long-term results to a heavy concentration on only the short term. Losing the strong values and culture that had made the company great resulted in the exit of large numbers of management. What had been a best team turned into a very dysfunctional one.

Another example of a great company gone wrong is Hewlett-Packard, which had once been one of the symbolic founders of Silicon Valley. Through the 1990s, Hewlett-Packard was a leader in personal computers and printers. Similar to Motorola, Hewlett-Packard enjoyed a strong heritage of internally driven innovation. However, when Hewlett-Packard's innovation engine stalled, it began to rely on acquisitions to drive growth, which changed the culture and the focus of the company. For example, it purchased Compaq Computer after a lengthy and heated proxy battle; however, incompatible values and a poor strategic rationale undermined that deal. Another failed acquisition was Autonomy, purchased for $11 billion in 2011; within a year, $9 billion of the acquisition price was written off. In terms of leadership, the company went through four CEOs from 2000 to 2012. From a high of $70 a share in 2000, Hewlett-Packard has fallen to $20 currently—a reduction of more than 70 percent.

Damaged values and a dysfunctional culture can also result when an organization is undermined by its own success. In the beginning, the right people are brought in; they think and act consistently with the organization's principles and values. But as the enterprise grows and does well, it can become a victim of its good fortune. First, the company starts reading its own press clippings, those laudatory reports of how great the enterprise is and how the leaders just can't go wrong. People in the organization convince themselves that their success speaks for itself. Clearly, they've got *the* model. As the organization generates solid returns, leaders believe the company can be put on autopilot—it can practically run itself.

What keeps a best team running smoothly is feedback, which continuously aligns people to the values of the organization and its clear, elevating goals. Members of a best team are always challenging each other to improve; people are constantly being developed with open communication and honest feedback. The best team never reads its own press clippings. They don't rest on their laurels, because they know that the bigger their sandbox gets, the more attractive it is to someone else who wants to stake their claim. The moment a company becomes complacent, things can fall apart, and what had been a great company will start to tarnish.

A third scenario occurs when a company that has been doing well with good organic growth, suddenly experiences a slowdown. In order to keep the momentum going, the company decides to pursue external growth through acquisitions, including outside its area of core competencies or strong suit. (Jim Collins, in the classic *Good to Great*, advocated that companies act like "hedgehogs," recalling an ancient Greek parable that says foxes know many small things and hedgehogs know one big thing. Similarly, good-to-great companies develop a "hedgehog concept" that is simple, but profoundly so—guiding the company forward and facilitating its decision-making.[2]) When a company ventures beyond its strengths, especially in a big way such as through a major acquisition, things can go wrong. Leaders who are no longer operating as their best selves and who don't engage in self-reflection can easily delude themselves. They tell themselves, "We were really successful doing X; I bet we can do Y really well, too!"

---

[2] Jim Collins, "Good to Great," *Fast Company*, October 2001. www.jimcollins.com/article_topics/articles/good-to-great.html.

This presents a problem on two levels. First, the company is so good at doing X, it is the market leader. But in Y, other companies are the leaders. Even if the company buys a Y contender, it won't have the same strengths in terms of technology, innovation, and people that it enjoys in X. And if that isn't a big enough problem, another trap is when the acquiring company doesn't closely examine the culture and values of the Y company it wants to buy. If the fit factor is an unknown until the deal is done, all too often, it turns out to be a negative surprise.

When one company buys another, or there is a *merger of equals* (an oxymoron, since only one company culture can realistically survive), what happens with the values? Suddenly Company A, a company with, say, 10,000 employees gains another 5,000 or 6,000 through the merger or acquisition. The Company B team leaders will be brought into the management circle since they are running what is now the B division in which the A team has little or no expertise. If there is a mismatch on values, the acquisition will likely fail on the fit factor alone. Then, fingers of blame are pointed across the Company A leadership team: *Why didn't we know this was going to be a mistake?* The reason is simple: Company A focused only on the numbers—the financial projection of what the returns *could* be if it expanded into a new area—but no one really focused on whether Company B's team operated under similar values-based principles as Company A.

The result is an acquisition that takes too long to integrate. The economies of scale, such as using a common distribution system, don't materialize as planned. Instead of applying best practices across a larger enterprise, turf wars break out.

In these scenarios, it ultimately comes down to a lack of self-reflection among the top leaders. When no one really takes into account whether the company stands to lose what made it great, the best team begins to crumble. Fortunately, there is a way to move from brokenness to best team: a complete turnaround in values.

TURNING AROUND AN ICON: CAMPBELL SOUP AND DOUG CONANT[3]

Douglas Conant is a best-self leader. He's a good friend (we've known each other for more than 15 years), and I admire him for what he stands for and his unwavering commitment to values-based leadership. Moreover, when it comes to real-world experience in turning around a team by starting with its values, a strong example is what Doug accomplished as president and CEO of the Campbell Soup Company from 2001 to 2011.

When Doug was brought in from Nabisco to lead Campbell—as the 11th CEO in its 141-year history—this iconic company was in the midst of significant challenges: declining performance, escalating competitive pressures, and a precipitous drop in market value. The root cause of the problem could be traced back to a decision in the early 1990s to aggressively raise prices. The price increases created a sizeable differential between Campbell's and other products, especially private-label store brands. This triggered a sales decline, which, in turn, led to the decision to significantly reduce advertising and promotional spending. With sales and earnings now at risk, the company aggressively cut costs in a variety of ways, going so far as to compromise the quality of its most iconic varieties. When Doug was recruited into the company in the aftermath of these poor decisions, he summed it up succinctly in an interview with the *Financial Times*: "After taking the pricing up, cutting the marketing support, and compromising on product quality, [Campbell] started to cut the overhead including hundreds of R&D people, the lifeblood of a consumer-products company."[4] In the aftermath of these actions,

---

[3] Douglas Conant, telephone interview, June 19, 2014. Related quotes and data regarding Campbell Soup Company come from this interview unless footnotes indicate otherwise.

[4] Jim Champy, "Getting Back to Focus and Discipline: Campbell's Soup Is M'M M'M Smart," *FT Press*, August 24, 2011. www.ftpress.com/articles/article.aspx?p=1745739.

9 out of 10 people "had lost a best friend at work," Doug noted, and the culture had become toxic.

To top it all off, between 1997 and 2000, sales of condensed soup dropped more than 20 percent. In the midst of poor performance, the company had lost half of its market value and many of its best employees, and there were added concerns about allegedly questionable business practices.

The most telling sign of just how dismal things were at the Campbell Soup Company was an employee engagement ratio revealed by a Gallup Organization survey of employees: for every two employees who were engaged, one was not. Essentially, one-third of Campbell's employees were disengaged from the company and their responsibilities. Among Campbell's top leaders, the ratio was even worse: 1.6 to 1. Taking over in 2001, Doug and his team set about to dramatically improve these ratios (which he did, eventually surpassing world-class standards). With the rallying cry of "it's not enough to be a legend," Doug drew upon his personal principles and leadership values to bring about a turnaround at Campbell by reigniting a best team.

Our conversation centered on the values-based approach Doug took to successfully recreate and re-energize a best team at Campbell. His endeavors at Campbell mirrored what I've witnessed and experienced in my own career as a leader: people operating as their best selves as part of a best team inspire confidence. Everyone knows that, on a best team, people are aligned with the mission and values of the organization. This is critical to establishing consistency within a values-based organization. After all, as Doug observes, most decisions are made when the leader is not in the room. From the heads of divisions and departments, down to the folks in the cubicles who are closest to the customers, individual contributors act on their own, day in and day out, on behalf of the organization. The risk of aberrant or inconsistent behavior is huge, unless people are part of a best team that is grounded in consistent values.

"To me, it's all about people, and how they are representing you and the enterprise when you are not in the room, which is about 99 percent of the time," Doug says in our conversation. "With this realization, you need to have highly competent, high-character people—the right people on the bus, in the right seat, and with the right motivation."

That is the essence of a best team: strong in competence, character, and teamwork. Recruiting, developing, and retaining people who are operating at a high level—as their best selves— enables the company to leverage that highly skilled and valuable talent. As teams perform at their optimal levels, so does the enterprise, even to the point of outperforming its peers.

Form, Storm, Norm, and Perform

To create his best team, Doug started with a powerful, yet simple team-building concept: *form, storm, norm, and perform.*[5] To execute using this concept, he had to *form* a high-performance team that could *storm* through the issues, set the *norm* for high expectations, and ultimately *perform* at the highest levels. "When you go into a turnaround, the first thing you have to do is help the team understand what's expected in terms of the goals," Doug explains.

"You have to have high standards for performance. You can never compromise," he adds. "It's a slippery slope to mediocrity. Clearly, those standards need to be competitive and aspirational, but also approachable."

Doug formed and declared the goal of a three-year turnaround process, telling his team, "It took the company several years to get into this mess, it will take us three years to get out of it in a quality way." As he recalls, "You can't talk your way out of something you behaved your way into. You have to behave your way out of it."

"We were disciplined, we had resolve," Doug adds. "However, quite candidly, with all the change, I was concerned that I was going to blow up the company. On the other hand, I felt that I had no choice. We had to deliver quality results and to do it in an enduring

[5] B. W. Tuckman, "Development Sequence in Small Groups," *Psychological Bulletin* 63 (1965): 384-399.

way—by inspiring trust, valuing people, and focusing on perform-ance. The team had to deliver." Before the team could deliver, however, team members had to be re-engaged. From Campbell's abysmal employee engagement ratings, the world-class standard of 12-to-1 must have seemed light years away.

In order to stage a successful turnaround, Doug had to over-haul the culture. "You've got to declare yourself day one, and then walk the talk every day," he says. "As a leader, once you declare what you are going to deliver and how you are going to deliver it, everybody is going to be watching 24/7."

WALKING THE TALK—LITERALLY

Doug led the transformation to turn around employee engage-ment at Campbell Soup Company in numerous ways, big and small, all of them significant, and all of them collectively impactful. He sent a strong message early on by setting clear expectations for how leaders would behave—both in terms of setting and meeting goals, as well as expectations of leadership profile. Leaders received performance feedback every six months to monitor what was working and what was not. Within three years, 300 leaders who were not delivering on the newly established expectations left the company. Jim Champy, a journalist who covered Doug's tenure as Campbell's CEO notes in the *Financial Times*:

> *On the face of it, Doug Conant's decision to dismiss 300 of Campbell's 350 top people may seem extreme. . . . But drastic action was needed to right the company. What ails many organizations is the commitment of current management to dysfunctional behaviors. . . . Often, that commitment is so strong that it is virtually impossible for its believers to embrace new ways of operating.[6]*

[6] Jim Champy, "Getting Back to Focus and Discipline: Campbell's Soup Is M'M M'M Smart," *FT Press*, August 24, 2011. www.ftpress.com/articles/article.aspx? p=1745739.

Doug gave those who truly supported the turnaround a reason to have hope and regain confidence. He took the tough actions, acknowledged when and where things did not work, celebrated successes, and shared credit with the team he had formed around core principles and aligned values. As he forged his new leadership team, he found 150 deserving candidates in the next tier (below the 300 who were let go) and promoted them. The company then hired another 150 leaders, many of them from well-regarded consumer packaged-goods companies, who had the capacity to do what was needed to transform Campbell. Real change was beginning to happen, as the results would soon show.

Doug didn't just work in broad strokes; he also used finesse— and a fountain pen. Over the course of his 10 years as CEO, he handwrote no fewer than 30,000 personal notes to the company's 20,000 employees, acknowledging significant contributions. These acknowledgments became treasures to the team members who received them.

Another powerful way in which Doug acknowledged and engaged team members was by walking around. This was not just a short stroll on the executive floor; he often logged 10,000 steps per day. *Management by walking around* (or *wandering around*, as it's also called) has a long history, and was popularized by management guru Tom Peters, among others. The concept is that leaders can become more engaged with their team members by becoming highly visible, walking around the workplace, and interacting with people. In impromptu and informal ways, leaders can hear problems, discuss solutions, acknowledge team efforts, and send a very clear message that they are committed to making themselves available.

By literally *walking the talk*, Doug observed people in action, engaged individuals and teams, fielded questions, acknowledged successes, and discussed problems and concerns. In short, whatever was on the minds of team members he engaged with became *his* priority at that moment. Through this practice, Doug modeled the type of behavior he wanted to see throughout the organization—people actively engaged in the company's success.

"You have to have a good, trusting working relationship with the people who have your back when you're not in the room," Doug says. Doing that effectively means prioritizing both standards and people—being tough-minded with the standards, and tender-hearted with the people. He explains, "The leadership team needs to bring balance to the equation. They need to have high standards—find the 'busted numbers' in the spreadsheets—but also celebrate the people and their contributions in meaningful ways, whenever possible."

This kind of granular leader–team engagement is crucial to forming a best team. Think about it: When a best team exists, people feel that they are truly part of something bigger. There is a clear, aspirational goal, and people feel motivated to do whatever it takes—within a specific department, division, region, geography, or level—to make it happen. Moreover, they know that what they do truly matters to their bosses (and their bosses' bosses), the division president, all the way up to the CEO. They know it, because they see and hear the evidence from the leaders who are visibly walking around.

A leader might stop by a cubicle to say hello, or pop in on a team meeting to see how things are going. Maybe it's to remind someone of the Friday night company softball game, or to inquire about someone's new baby or a sick parent. Through genuine, sincere interaction team members know that they are seen and valued as individuals, and that what they do matters. This feeling of validation spreads throughout the organization, encouraging others to adopt the attitude that *we're all in this together*. A team member who feels validated is far more apt to pitch in and help another colleague or a different team on their project, because they're all focused on serving customers.

"The CEO is really the *chief engagement officer*, spending 80 percent of his/her time making sure the organization has the best imaginable talent in the best imaginable positions, with the best imaginable alignment," Doug says. "It's all about the people and their engagement."

Re-energizing the team is also part of what Doug calls "building the emotional bank account of the organization." This account contains such things as a best-team attitude, employee validation, ethical behavior, faith that top leadership is competent and of high character, and an overarching commitment to the team and its performance in very real and tangible ways. However, there are so many ways this account can get depleted: the constant sniping of disgruntled employees, complaints from unsatisfied customers, and criticism from activist groups. Anything that goes wrong gets blasted across the headlines and the enterprise. Little by little, these debits eat into the emotional bank account, which, if not replenished with positive actions, will run into the red. "These withdrawals are happening every day," Doug says. "You have to keep the balance of this account in the black in a clear-eyed and responsible way, so people can feel good about the organization in a clear-eyed and responsible way."

The time to make these deposits is not after the fact, when some crisis has hit the company. Rather, the balance must be increased proactively, before problems surface or challenges occur.

WINNING ON FOUR DIMENSIONS

As part of the turnaround, the Campbell leadership team determined that the company needed to win on four dimensions: in the workplace with engaged team members, in the marketplace with measurable growth, in the community with a strategically focused social agenda, and across all three of those dimensions with integrity. Winning in the workplace *must* come first, before the organization can hope to win in the marketplace in a sustainable fashion. That means, before the team can be expected to demonstrate their commitment to the company and its goals and expectations, the company must demonstrate its commitment to the team. This became the basis of the Campbell Promise: "Campbell valuing people, people valuing Campbell."

"People need to make a living, to feel valued and loved, to have opportunities to learn, and ultimately to believe that they are doing something special," Doug says. "It's incumbent upon leaders to create that special environment where all four of those need states are addressed while delivering a quality performance." Only when team members are highly engaged and performing at their highest level, can the enterprise expect to gain competitive advantage, enlarge market share, increase margins, improve profitability, and, ultimately, generate shareholder value in a sustainable way.

Inside the Campbell Turnaround

During Doug's first three years at Campbell, from 2001 to 2004, the team worked at achieving internal change. They redefined the corporate culture, which helped identify which leaders were on board with the changes to the Campbell workplace. Anyone who wasn't (including those 300 or so leaders mentioned earlier) was let go and replaced with people who shared the organization's new vision and ethos. Coupled with Doug's management style, these changes boosted employee engagement and productivity.

From 2005 to 2008, the team shifted its focus to Campbell's customers. Like the company's employees, consumers had also disengaged from the brand. To regain their customers' trust, Doug and his team recognized that they had to deliver a high-quality product that was a good value. In some cases, this meant going back to the old way of doing things. In other cases, it meant listening to consumers and developing new products to meet their needs. Regaining the brand's competitive edge also meant taking another look at Campbell's prices to give customers the value they wanted.

The final stage of the turnaround started in 2008. According to the plan, if everything had been well executed, Campbell could expect to bounce back to once again become a market leader and a household favorite.[7]

With a strongly engaged best team, financial results greatly improved, bringing consistent gains in earnings per share, organic sales growth that was twice the average of the food industry, record high return on investment capital (ROIC), and strong cash flow. "But that's only part of the story," Doug says. "In order to sustainably deliver the best financial performance, just having good financial numbers is insufficient. It's how we engaged employees in order to keep the financial engine going in a quality way."

A win cannot be declared based merely on what a leader notices or feels. A leader can't walk around one day and decide that people *seem* happier; there must be quantifiable evidence. By 2007, Campbell's employee engagement ratio (as measured by the Gallup Organization) had increased to 9-to-1; by July 2008, it had reached the top rating of 12-to-1. But it didn't stop there. In 2009, employee engagement at the company hit a stellar level of 23-to-1, meaning 82 percent of people at the company were engaged with their work, happy, and productive. Among the top 350 leaders, engagement skyrocketed from the dismal 2001 level of 1.6-to-1, to 77-to-1 in 2010—a level so high, the Gallup Organization had never recorded the likes of it before.

Looking back, Doug speaks with admiration for his team and gratitude for what was achieved, but it's no real surprise that these strongly positive results were achieved. "We got the right people on the bus. We set the norms for business performance and leaders' performance, and we held people accountable," he says. In short, a best team was in place.

[7]Jim Champy, "Getting Back to Focus and Discipline: Campbell's Soup Is M'M M'M Smart," *FT Press*, August 24, 2011. www.ftpress.com/articles/article.aspx?p=1745739.

Winning in the Workplace, Marketplace, and Community

As employee engagement improved, the quality of the Campbell Soup workplace was widely recognized. For example, it received the Catalyst Award for its efforts to create an inclusive work environment and expand opportunities for women.

Just as Doug had predicted, as engagement rose and the workplace improved, so did returns in the marketplace—making the new corporate culture a win for the company and shareholders as well. The measure here was total shareholder returns (TSRs), including stock appreciation and dividends, relative to the peer group. Measuring the period from July 2004 to July 2010, when Doug's retirement was announced, Campbell's TSR was 64 percent, well above the 38 percent average of the S&P Packaged Foods index (and far better than the 13.1 percent of the S&P 500 index overall).

Winning in the community meant operating in a socially responsible manner. Campbell promoted sustainable farming and manufacturing practices, and made a major commitment to Camden, New Jersey, where the company was founded, including building a $70 million corporate campus in the economically depressed city. It also sponsored several programs to educate and train young people, revitalize neighborhoods, support health clinics, and provide meals. Once again, Campbell achieved a lofty goal—this time, to be recognized as one of the most socially responsible U.S. companies. In fiscal year 2010, for the second year in a row, the Boston College Center for Corporate Citizenship and the Reputation Institute ranked Campbell as one of the 10 most socially responsible U.S. companies, along with the likes of Intel, Google, and Disney. "And we were an old economy soup company based in the poorest, most dangerous city in the U.S.!" Doug exclaims.

Other honors included recognition for employee volunteerism by the Points of Light Institute; being named one of the 100 Best Corporate Citizens by *Corporate Responsibility* magazine; and inclusion in the Dow Jones Sustainability Index (North America) and the Dow Jones Sustainability World Index. In 2010, *Ethisphere* magazine named Campbell one of the world's most ethical companies. "It was all enabled by people: a leadership team that was engaged in a fulsome turnaround," Doug says. "I can't imagine delivering that kind of performance without having the right people in the room making the right decisions when I wasn't there."

As Doug penned his shareholders' letter for the 2010 annual report, there was no doubt that the turnaround had occurred at all levels. Doug was also preparing for his retirement at the end of fiscal year 2011. "As I reflect on my time with Campbell, I am very pleased with our progress in the workplace, the marketplace, and the community," the letter reads. "When I arrived, Campbell was among the worst performing companies in the industry. The company had failed on a number of fronts. While it remained an American icon, Campbell had lost touch with its consumers, investors had begun to lose faith, and, as you can imagine, employee morale was low."[8]

A best team is never about just one individual, no matter how dynamic or talented. As Doug's retirement neared, a highly capable successor was named: Denise Morrison, who had been executive vice president and chief operating officer, and a company director, in anticipation that she would become CEO at the beginning of fiscal year 2012.

"They're doing even better since I left," Doug says. Those words carried the pride he still has for the enduring success of the best team he helped to create, which still carries the torch of values-based leadership in their own authentic way.

THE TURNAROUND LEADER

When a company is broken, a turnaround is needed. But, as Doug Conant and his work at Campbell Soup Company show, it's not just a matter of cutting costs, improving efficiencies, increasing the

---

[8] Campbell Soup Company, Fiscal 2010 Annual Report.

profit margin, or some other financial target. Companies achieve their results through people. When individuals operate as their best selves they are capable of forming best teams. With a best team, individual contributions are compounded, as people bring out the best in themselves, in each other, and from the team as a whole. Across an organization, a cultural turnaround toward a best-team atmosphere is a powerful rebirth.

The catalyst is the leader who is deeply committed to values-based leadership. Using the principles of self-reflection, balance and perspective, true self-confidence, and genuine humility, a leader can orchestrate a complete transformation. But the task is daunting. It takes a special talent—even among values-based leaders—to turn around a company, especially a large organization with tens of thousands of team members.

To engage in such a challenge, a values-based leader must dig deep and engage in self-reflection, which is always the first and most important tool in the values-based leadership toolbox. Through self-reflection, the values-based leader stays grounded in the task-at-hand, the incremental progress being made, and the challenges that remain.

This means digging deep and being completely honest with one's self: *Am I capable of leading this turnaround? Do I listen to others and their viewpoints, so that I have balance and perspective? Do I have enough true self-confidence in my abilities? Do I have the genuine humility to admit that I'm a little scared and I can't do this by myself? Do I have strong enough communication skills?* Only by being his or her best self can a leader hope to be successful.

The turnaround of a company, as people rediscover their best selves and re-engage as best teams, is inspiring. It demonstrates what can be done with vision, commitment, and resolve. At the same time, it is also a cautionary tale. Nothing has the potential to breed failure more than success. As companies become successful, it is easy for organizations, just as it is for individuals, to lose genuine humility. The entire organization, from the leaders on down, move from true self-confidence to false confidence. The culture becomes one in which people forget where they came from. People start reading their own press clippings and believing them. While they are busy patting themselves on the back, rivals that previously found it difficult to compete with this great company suddenly begin to bypass it.

The moral of the story is that, while a turnaround in culture is possible, it's best to avoid the need for one altogether by never losing sight of the *bests*—starting with the first two: the best self and the best team. Building on these strong foundational elements, companies can secure their present and move more confidently toward the future.

CHAPTER 4

CREATING A BEST TEAM FROM SCRATCH

E ntrepreneurs start with a dream and an idea. They have a solution to a problem within an industry, or a concept for a product that consumers don't even know they want (but hopefully soon will). If the idea is truly breakthrough, it will be a *disruptor*, shaking up how business is done or customers are served. The results could be revolutionary.

At the very beginning, a start-up company is usually just an entrepreneur and maybe a partner or two. There is no infrastructure or formalized process—sometimes there's not even an office. Some of the most successful companies got their start in a college dorm room (e.g., Facebook, Dell computers) or a garage (e.g., Amazon, Google, Apple, Tesla). When the digital world talks about a *lean* start-up, they're not kidding—it's bare bones for a long time.

If what I observe in my classes at Northwestern University's Kellogg School of Management is any indication, the entrepreneurial world will continue to attract young business leaders and their breakthrough ideas. When I was a Kellogg student 35 years ago, at least 95 percent of us planned to work for large established companies. Our goal was to join well-known firms such as Ford,

IBM, General Electric, and Bank of America. Today, when I ask my students how many of them want to be entrepreneurs and start their own companies, at least 70 to 80 percent raise their hands. Even among those who say they want to work for larger companies, many plan to be there only two or three years to gain some insights before going off on their own.

While entrepreneurs focus on their concepts or ideas, that's really not the key to success. Ultimately, start-ups require a best team composed of people who not only have a particular skill set (and risk tolerance), but who are also aligned around common values, such as being their best selves. In this chapter, we'll focus on how a best team is built from scratch in an entrepreneurial environment with many moving parts and competing priorities, using the exciting start-up Fieldglass as an example.

THE LEADER'S VALUES

In a large company, there are departments and divisions. Teams are in place and the culture has been established. Even if it needs to be overhauled, as described in Chapter 3, there is a track record of performance. With a start-up, however, it's a blank slate. Everything must be established by the founder. The danger, however, is that there are so many pieces to be put into place, the entrepreneur may not devote sufficient time to defining the company's values. Or, the assumption may be that the values are something that can happen down the road, when the company is well established. In a startup, having a best team cannot be put off until the company is bigger or until it has passed some critical point when existence is no longer in question. Having a best team matters from the moment the first person joins the founder. This is where culture starts: how people treat others, internally and externally, how they do business, what they stand for, what matters most.

In a start-up, the core values of the enterprise are the core values of the founder. It starts with how the leader acts, not just what he or she says. If the leader says one thing and does another, then all the talk is meaningless. What the leader feels most strongly about must be demonstrated and communicated clearly, whether the company is a two-person team or has scaled to 20,000 team members.

If you are an entrepreneur, you must first be your best self. Your best self is *not* an initial phase; it is the foundation that must continue to stay strong, supporting all of the other bests. Through self-reflection, you find out what your values are—ideally, putting them in writing for yourself and, later, for your team. This exercise is as important for you, as an entrepreneur, as all the brainstorming you do at a whiteboard. Defining values means giving serious thought to such questions as what means the most to you, and what standards will you never compromise.

"As the leader, you have to tell people what your values are," says Gary Gorman, founder of Gorman & Co. Inc., a real-estate development company based in Wisconsin.[1] I've known Gary since our undergraduate college days at Lawrence University. I respect him as a successful entrepreneur, and as someone who truly lives his values as his best self.

His firm's core value is also Gary's personal value: "We protect our reputation at all costs." Commitment to it is total, such that during the real estate and financial crises that started in 2007, Gorman & Co. never walked away from its obligations. "In our 30 years we never defaulted on anything," Gary says.

Instead of letting lenders foreclose on an unprofitable development, or backing out of promises made to a community to reduce costs, taking the high road probably cost Gary's company "many millions." On a strictly bottom-line basis, keeping those commitments might have been a "bad" business decision—but only when viewed through the lens of short-term profits. "I believe that

---

[1] Gary Gorman, telephone interview, June 25, 2014. Quotes and data regarding Gorman & Co. come from this interview unless footnotes indicate otherwise.

long-term, people with good reputations will be successful," Gary says. As a values-based leader who is committed to being his best self and fostering best teams, Gary cannot act any other way.

At some point in a fledgling business's life cycle, that small, but powerful nucleus consisting of the founder and a couple of other people must grow in order for a concept to turn into a company. It's still going to be lean, and people will be performing multiple roles, but as the firm grows from 2 people to 10 to 50 and so on, a team must be built, with people who have not only the passion and skill set to rise to the entrepreneurial challenge, but also the right values.

So what's the secret to building a team of people who are aligned with the founder's values? Gary's advice is to communicate the values of the organization right from recruitment and hiring, and through the onboarding process, but there is no perfect system to screen for cultural fit. Once someone is on the job and facing pressure, that's when the truth comes out as to how well that person is aligned with the organization's values. Some people will work out better than others. "Be willing to screen out those who do not fit," Gary says.

Another element of the entrepreneur's values is the attitude toward risk. To expend the huge amounts of time, money, and energy necessary to launch a start-up, you have to believe in your idea enough to bet the farm on it. If things work out as planned, you may succeed. If things don't, you could suffer substantial losses. Before entering into the venture, you have to get comfortable with the possibility of loss. Self-reflection helps you look beyond the rose-colored glasses and provide a clearer look at the worst-case scenario and what you could stand to lose: your savings, your house, your car. If you can handle that risk, then everything else is upside. But if the mere thought of that loss makes you sick to your stomach, then you can't handle the risk, and the entrepreneurial path is probably not for you.

Similarly, to launch your company, you will need to attract people who are aware of the risks and are willing to take them, provided that there is potential to make a substantial reward. But this is where the straight talk comes in, which should be part of the entrepreneur's value system. Recruiting people for a start-up means telling them about the risks as well as the rewards: *We think we have a great idea here, but if we don't attract customers, then we're out of luck. If you can't deal with that possibility, then this isn't the place for you.* For those who are willing to move beyond their comfort zones, who can take the bruises and put in the hours doing their own jobs and a dozen more besides that, then the entrepreneurial journey can be the adventure of a lifetime.

FROM THE START: A BEST TEAM

Jai Shekhawat has joined the ranks of highly successful entrepreneurs whose great ideas not only scaled from concept to company, but also attracted the attention of a much bigger organization. His company, Fieldglass, was sold to SAP, the German technology company, in mid-2014. (The transaction price was not disclosed, but media reports have put it at more than $1 billion.[2])

Fieldglass, which Jai established in 1999, offers a *vendor management system* (VMS) for the procurement of contract labor and services. As Ernst & Young observes in a case study, Fieldglass "has become the industry leader in helping companies manage their contingent workforce—not by offering something entirely new, but by building a sustainable competitive advantage." That advantage marries streamlined procurement of temporary workers and outsourced services with cloud technology. As Jai saw it, the contingent labor market needed to adopt a "supply-chain perspective of talent," making it easier for hiring managers to evaluate talent and process requisitions, and for suppliers to plan for demand.[3]

[2] John Pletz, "John Pletz on Technology: Big as in Billion," *Crain's Chicago Magazine*, May 9, 2014. www.chicagobusiness.com/article/20140509/BLOGS11/140509783/big-as-in-billion-fieldglass-sale-topped-1-000-000-000.

[3] Ernst & Young, "Fieldglass," *Exceptional Magazine*, Americas edition, July 2013. www.ey.com/US/en/Services/Strategic-Growth-Markets/Exceptional-magazine-Americas-edition-July-2013—Fieldglass.

At the time of the sale to SAP, Fieldglass had approximately 350 employees. Its cloud-based VMS solutions are used in more than 100 countries. For his success in launching and scaling Fieldglass, Jai was named Ernst & Young's 2012 Midwest Entrepreneur of the Year, and received the 2012 Peter Yessne Staffing Innovator Award as a pioneer in VMS technology.

Earlier in his career, Jai had been a strategy consultant with McKinsey & Company, and had worked as a senior executive at Syntel, a software services firm. He had co-founded Quinnox, a technology and business solutions firm. With Fieldglass, Jai hoped to transform an existing industry—a tremendous task that would require a best team from day one, amidst all the other priorities and pressures of launching a business.

"The first problem with creating a start-up is the element of time," Jai explains. "The second is you lack infrastructure. You have no one, and yet you have to go out and meet customers. The third is you have to make things happen—to make a product."[4]

With this backdrop of challenges, Jai decided that his best team would begin with two people: someone to build the product and someone to sell the product. He stayed away from looking for specific titles—a VP of finance or a chief technology officer. Instead, he sought out people who were passionate about the business and capable of delivering what was expected.

The person he selected to build the product was a project manager—not a job title that would be the logical choice. But when Jai looked at the whole person, he saw someone who, earlier in his life, had been a Marine rifleman. This resonated with Jai because his father had been an officer in the Indian Navy. "I knew that this guy had a can-do attitude and would fight to the end," Jai recalls. "He would do whatever it took, not just to get the job done, but to accomplish the mission."

---

[4]Jai Shekhawat, telephone interview, June 25, 2014. Quotes and data regarding Fieldglass come from this interview unless footnotes indicate otherwise.

For the person who was in charge of selling the product, Jai also chose an individual with a military background—facilitating night landings on aircraft carriers—which, as Jai observes, "takes some spine."

From that team of three, the company began. "The three of us were in lock step. We bonded and traveled together. The rest of the team formed around us," Jai says. "We had a can-do culture."

As the Fieldglass team expanded, not every person who joined the company was a perfect fit. For example, early on, someone in a functional role, who had been recommended by venture capitalists backing the firm (they wanted *their guy* on the team), came from a big-company environment. He was an excellent manager and used to delegating, but not as strong in doing the work himself—or pitching in to help out wherever he was needed. The lack of fit meant he had to be phased out quickly. It wasn't personal; in fact, nothing related to a best team should be personal. "Rather, it's all about the edifice called the company," Jai says. "If you can create the externality that everyone is working for the purpose of building a great company, then it's easier to make a termination in service of that externality."

When the team is small, fit is crucial. If one person is not aligned with the values or the culture, the negative impact is exponential. Therefore, it is the leader's job to strive for the best fit possible when it comes to making hires. Although no one's track record is 100 percent, a leader who devotes the time and attention to screening candidates thoroughly will do better than most.

Mark Thierer, chairman and CEO of Catamaran Corporation, one of the largest pharmacy benefit managers in the United States (see Chapter 6), takes pride in how he has built a best team among the top twelve people who form the core of the organization. "I recruited most of them personally. I spent anywhere from a half day to two days of 'immersion time' with each of them before I hired them, with extended dinners that often included their spouses," Mark says. "I do between five and eight reference checks for each person, and I do them myself—even to this day."

Mark believes the care he takes in making hires "casts a large shadow" in the organization, modeling for others how crucial it is to identify the best people for the team and ensuring that someone is a good fit for the culture. Because of the process of personally handpicking talent, he adds, "I'd put our team up against anyone in the industry."

TEAM FIRST, EGO LAST

From the founder and CEO to every member of the team, what's needed is a "subordination of ego," Jai says, which he sees as fundamental to the philosophy of servant leadership. The leader serves the team, and together they devote their service to the mission and vision of the organization. Jai credits this servant leadership attitude to his father who, as a naval officer, "truly thought of himself as a servant of his country." Similarly, as Jai established his best team, he modeled the attitude that "we are servants of the thing we are building, but only if we give this thing— the company—supremacy. Only then could we succeed."

Jai's model of servant leadership and subordination of ego certainly runs contrary to some icons of entrepreneurship who have built hugely successful companies from scratch without self-reflection. As a result, their companies are all about them. It's hard to reconcile notions of true leadership with the idea of a humble servant CEO, particularly when stories in the media celebrate people with giant egos who create amazing companies. On that basis alone, you might wonder if arrogance and egotism are really what it takes to be a successful entrepreneur, and not this values-based leadership stuff. It's a question I'm frequently asked in my classes.

All I can offer is my theory about these outliers. These people are so bright, so gifted, that even though they are not values-based leaders and do not treat others as part of a best team, they can override these failings. They are so unique—occupying a place way out there in terms of vision and talent, beyond three standard deviations from the norm—that they are successful, in spite of themselves.

Then, there are the rest of us. We have creative ideas of how to satisfy customers' needs or to do things in a new, improved way. If we do not act as our best selves or if we do not embrace the importance of a best team, we are going to fail. We can't think that we're one of those one-in-a-million creative geniuses for whom the world will make an exception.

Here's where true self-confidence and genuine humility form a partnership in service of the entrepreneur. As we recall from Chapter 2, there is never a trade-off between these two principles of values-based leadership; you never need more of one at the expense of the other. You always need more of both.

As a values-based leader and entrepreneur, you need true self-confidence, and you had better know what you know and what you don't know, or else your venture will never get off the ground. True self-confidence empowers you to recognize the uniqueness of your proposition so you can sell it with confidence and authenticity to customers. In the case of Fieldglass, that meant knowing that "the existing contingent workforce structure needed to be disrupted, and we were the ones to do it," Jai says. "It was an important movement. I framed it in a compelling way."

Genuine humility affirms the value of every single person, and communicates that no one is more important than anyone else. Everyone is aligned with a common mission: the success of the organization. With genuine humility and true self-confidence, Jai created a unique, mission-focused approach to sales. Rather than trying to get customers to buy a particular product, Jai told them, "I am here to ask for your problem. Sharing your problem with me would be the greatest gift. In return, I will give you a solution that may involve a product."

FROM LAUNCH TO SCALE

As the start-up moves from its initial launch phase to its first years of growth, it may see some changes in its best team. Some people may move on to new opportunities; others will be filtered out because they don't fit with the values of the growing organization. Other changes will happen organically because of the skill sets needed to grow the organization. As part of creating and sustaining the best team for scaling the firm, the entrepreneur/leader also must be self-reflective enough to ask himself honestly if he has what it takes to truly be a CEO.

To illustrate this issue, Jai divides the priorities of a growing start-up into three "buckets." The first relates to the idea itself—the concept that makes the business unique. The second encompasses all people issues, and the third contains the financing and money-related matters. "All our problems ended up being a combination and interface of these three—for example, if the idea stops being compelling, people will leave and no one will fund you," Jai explains.

The three are managed effectively with a best-team approach—having the right people for the job, starting at the top. Jai distinguishes between the entrepreneur who founded the business and the CEO who runs the operation day to day. Sometimes the roles can be occupied by the same person, but not always. The entrepreneur who is the idea-generator may not be able to execute a "functioning, defensible business model," which includes such complexities as production, pricing, sales, and support functions. Because of his background in corporate strategy, consulting, and outsourcing, and the skill set he had acquired, Jai believed he was the right person to be both the founder and the CEO of Fieldglass.

Of primary importance for the CEO of a start-up, Jai said, is to ensure that the business idea is a sound one. While there are no guarantees for any start-up, as the CEO, Jai had "a strong moral responsibility not to take two or three people out of their lives to join me unless I had something defensible." Only from this belief in the business could he recruit his best team.

"Human beings tend to get excited about the possibility of doing big, important things," Jai says. "Psychologically, this is more appealing than saying to someone, 'Come to work for me as a programmer.'"

Balance and perspective encourage input from others; genuine humility fosters an appreciation that no one has a monopoly on good ideas. Relying on these principles of values-based leadership, the CEO puts his best team to work on the business model. "This gives you more heads to solve the problems," Jai says. "But the CEO needs to subordinate his ego." In other words, the entrepreneur may be the one with the idea, but it takes a team of strong people with complementary talents to develop that idea into a marketable product or solution.

Some business leaders may prefer to have the strategy in place so that they can try to hire the people who fit that approach. The problem as I see it is, without the people, how can there be a workable strategy? A start-up's success, ultimately, is about hiring the right people from the start. This initial, core group typically becomes the heart and soul of the organization; they support one another, pitch in where help is needed, and share their skills and expertise freely. If this best team is not present from the beginning, it's impossible to pull out of the starting gate. You need "all hands on deck," as the saying goes, because there aren't that many of them. There is no time for seminars and formal training. It's just you, the founder, and a few other people who are working 24/7, figuring things out as you go.

"Everyone needs to contribute to the DNA of the firm we are creating," Jai says. "A person who is contributing and feels that they've helped shape the company will treat it like their child. These are the roots of loyalty."

Loyalty translates into ownership, which means more than getting a piece of the proverbial pie through stock options.

Ownership is emotional. It is the attitude that this is *my* company, whether I'm the owner, one of the original partners, the 10th hire, or the 500th person to join. The concept of having pride as an *owner* of the organization should extend to the mature enterprise as well. Even if the company is publicly traded and has 50,000 employees, each person should have pride of ownership, because they see the organization as *their company*.

An attitude of ownership also helps the best team to rally around the concept that organizations exist to serve customers. If there are no customers, then there's no company! Jai gave the example of *software as a service*, which in the tech world is called *SaaS*. Jai's best team approached this concept from the opposite direction: *service as software*. "The service has to be more central—it is service first," he said.

Fieldglass's service-first concept also unified best teams across all functions—not only programmers, developers, and the sales team, but others such as the general counsel and controller. The challenge for every person was to think about his or her particular job function in terms of service first. This might translate into simpler or more flexible contracts, or a different pricing structure. Putting the customer first also transformed the Fieldglass organizational chart, putting the customer in the center, and drawing the organization around it. That means people in a variety of functions—developers, sales, legal, finance—have direct customer contact.

CREATING OUT-OF-THE-BOX THINKING

As we recall from our previous discussion, a best team is not composed of people who only *play nice* and never question each other. In a start-up in particular, people on a best team must challenge each other, which also helps generate out-of-the-box thinking. If the team plays it safe with the known approaches, creativity will be stymied, but with trust and mutual respect, a best team can challenge one another to new levels of innovation.

Fieldglass applied a concept called "feed forward," which takes a proactive approach to giving and receiving input and commentary. This is different from feedback, which is typically based on something that has already occurred and, therefore, has the potential to be interpreted as antagonistic or even hostile. Feed forward, however, addresses future events and interactions, which removes the emotional charge. For example, with feed forward, a person might comment, "In order for me to do my job effectively, what I need you to do is . . ."

The feed forward concept is very much in sync with how I view effective feedback, which should not appear to be random or arbitrary. Rather, when expectations have been set for specific behaviors or performance targets, feedback directly answers the question: *Did we do what we agreed to do?* It's hard for people to become sensitive or annoyed with feedback if they knew what was expected. When expectations have been clearly established ahead of time, feedback that focuses on results is more directed and specific. It's also less subjective, which means these types of discussions are less likely to break down into gripe sessions. Instead, the best team acknowledges what went right, what went wrong, and, most important, what can be done better or differently the next time. In this way feedback (or feed forward) strengthens a best team and enhances alignment around common goals and approaches.

THE PRE-MORTEM

The purpose of feedback (and feed forward) is providing input to individuals so they can be successful in future tasks. In a parallel vein, a *post-mortem* is an analysis of an event (e.g., an acquisition, merger, or other investment) that compares results with expectations. One of Jai's innovative, best-team approaches is his concept of *pre-mortem*, which turns the notion of the post-mortem on its head. In a post-mortem, the view is hindsight—what went wrong and why. A pre-mortem takes place before a major event and, as Jai describes it, looks at what *could* go wrong, and uses that predictive capacity to identify what can be changed while there is still time to preempt any negative results.

He gave the example of Fieldglass's pending integration with SAP of Germany, a much larger, multinational software company that in 2013 reported total revenue of nearly €17 billion. In *Crain's Chicago Business,* Jai describes the SAP deal a "dream exit," adding, "I couldn't have asked for a better outcome."[5] Over the years, Fieldglass attracted about $38 million in venture-capital backing. In late 2010, Madison Dearborn Partners invested more than $100 million to buy a majority stake in the company. The purchase by SAP generated an attractive return for all investors.

The most challenging part of any acquisition, however, is not the deal itself, but what follows: integration of one independent company into another. Even when companies are well matched in terms of values and culture, and complementary in technology platforms and product lines, the integration will cause issues and challenges. Doing a pre-mortem becomes strategically preventive. As Jai explains, "Let's assume a year has gone by and [the integration with SAP] has not gone well. From this [hypothesis] you can think of what the probable causes for failure would be, but before that happens—when you still have a chance to influence the outcome."

With the insights from the pre-mortem, Fieldglass can go into the integration better prepared and they are less likely to be surprised by a problem or upset. "That's how we are planning," Jai says. "If we can see where the cracks are, we can jump ahead of them, and give ourselves a fighting chance for success."

BEST TEAM, START TO FINISH

With an exit as successful as the SAP purchase, the Fieldglass best team can take a bow—one that it is all the more deserved when one

---

[5] John Pletz, "Big as in Billion: Fieldglass Sale Topped $1,000,000,000," *Crain's Chicago Business,* May 9, 2014.

considers the trials and tribulations it endured along the way. For example, by 2001, Verizon Wireless had become the company's first customer, but they needed to land a second one. At the time, Jai was also raising a third round of financing. By August 2001, the company had four to five months of cash available, but after the September 11th terrorist attacks, the business world was shell-shocked and venture capital began to dry up for start-ups, which are considered riskier than traditional investments. To make matters worse, Jai tore his Achilles tendon while playing squash and needed surgery. He did pitches to venture capital firms on crutches—so he wasn't exactly the robust, energetic founder investors were hoping to see.

Fieldglass's second customer was American International Group (AIG), which acquired one of Fieldglass's original prospects, American General Insurance Company. A string of major clients followed, including Allstate, GlaxoSmithKline, and Johnson & Johnson. By June 2003, Fieldglass had raised $17 million in a third round of funding.[6] Fieldglass made its first profit in 2006; in 2007, it doubled its client base, which was mostly blue-chip companies.[7]

Such war stories make for great reminiscing, but they also serve to point out the importance of a highly coordinated and supportive best team, which deserves to be rewarded at every stage. For example, at the time a stake in Fieldglass was sold to Madison Dearborn, Jai says, about $20 million was set aside as "transaction bonuses" for everyone as a thank you, in addition to full acceler-ated vesting. As Jai explains, "This was a way of saying to our entire team, I want to reward you *before* you have done all the things that I am hoping you will do"—namely, taking the company to the next level of development, which could attract a firm like SAP.

In Jai's view, the best team concept demanded that all team members be rewarded, no matter if someone had been with

[6] IVCA, "Fieldglass, Inc.," (no date). www.illinoisvc.org/fieldglass–inc.
[7] Ernst & Young, "Fieldglass," *Exceptional Magazine*, Americas edition, July 2013. www.ey.com/US/en/Services/Strategic-Growth-Markets/Exceptional-magazine-Americas-edition-July-2013—Fieldglass.

Fieldglass from the beginning or was a more recent hire. "You can't talk about a team and reward only a few individuals," he says. "After the sale to SAP, we called back our first employee and handed him a large check. He had been gone eight years, but he deserved every bit of it."

IT'S ALL ABOUT THE PEOPLE

A startup rises or falls on the strength of its people. If a best team is in place, one that is squarely focused on serving customers, the chances of success greatly increase. If the wrong people are hired—individuals who are not customer focused, who act like it's all about them, and/or who are not acting as their best selves in alignment with the values of the organization—then there is no way a best team can exist.

Having a best team is foundational to success in organizations of any size. For example, when I was CEO of Baxter International, I made sure our best-team culture meant that people in every function had a customer orientation. If I passed a conference room where 10 or 12 people were meeting, I'd pop in and talk with them about our customers. No matter if they were from human resources or information technology, I'd ask them to name three of our customers. Sometimes, the response would be a shocked look—what I call MEGO, short for *my eyes glaze over.* People who may have been with Baxter for 15 years, and were very good at their function, did not see how their daily job related to the overall mission and vision of the organization. As a result, they could not name a single customer.

In a start-up, no such silos can exist. If you're the finance guy or you work in engineering, you may find yourself packing boxes for a customer order. This is not just teamwork; it is *best-team* work, creating a culture that prides itself on doing whatever it takes to deliver innovative solutions and products to customers.

In our digital world, technological advances will no doubt take us to places we haven't yet envisioned. Yet the germs of these ideas probably already exist in entrepreneurial minds. Some are just daydreams, others are doodles on a drawing board, or haven't gotten past the talking stage. Bringing these ideas to life will require a best team of people acting and interacting as their best selves, in service of a bigger purpose and a grander mission and vision, to change the way people live, work, interact, communicate, or enjoy leisure.

As these start-ups grow and mature, other *bests* are necessary, including being a *best partner* to customers and suppliers, as we discuss in Chapter 5. But organizations, large or small, well-established or start-up, never stop being about the people with complementary strengths and the unwavering commitment to be their best selves—people who function in highly effective, empowered groups known as *best teams*.

BEST PARTNER

Instead of only doing business to obtain the necessary supplies or services, the priority becomes having a best partnership.

Having made progress toward becoming our best selves, and realizing that we can't do it without a best team, we are now at a point where we can really get some business done! At this stage, we recognize that, in order to have a successful enterprise—whether public or private, for-profit or not-for-profit—we need to expand our best-team concept to include external "best partners." Thus, we are poised to create a ripple effect from one best to the next—self, team, and now, partner.

Before we can turn our sights externally and pick those suppliers, manufacturers, engineers, distributors, and others who can help our organization reach its goals, we first need to look internally: How can our organization become a best partner capable of attracting parties that want to do business with us on a mutually beneficial, long-term basis? How do our values and business practices appeal to the kinds of partners we need: those who will be strategically aligned with us and our mission of satisfying our customers? In other words, how can we be viewed by other parties as *their* best partner, worthy of the commitment and collaboration required to make a meaningful difference in the marketplace?

Second, we recognize that, even with a best team in place internally, we cannot do everything ourselves. We must have partners that contribute to our organization in specific ways, whether by supplying raw material or providing engineering, research and development, distribution, sales, customer service, or other support.

Becoming a best partner and forming strategic relationships requires us to turn, once again, to our four values-based leadership principles of self-reflection, balance and perspective, true self-confidence, and genuine humility. We cannot jump to the stage of being a best partner without first taking the time, through self-reflection, to ensure that we, personally, are acting as our best selves and are forming and retaining best teams. We need balance and perspective to gather the necessary input across the organization about our need for partnerships and what we bring to the table as a strong partner. With true self-confidence, we recognize our unique value proposition—knowing that, unless we create value in the marketplace, we won't have a sustainable business. Finally, genuine humility allows us to recognize and appreciate the input of our partners, to put our organizational egos aside to pursue collaboration with other entities that are stronger where we have weaknesses.

By employing the principles of values-based leadership, we gain deeper insight into what our organization stands for, our strategic strengths, and what we need to further enhance our value proposition in the eyes of consumers. This end-user orientation is as important for a not-for-profit (e.g., a philanthropic organization) as it is for a company in the business of selling a product or service. Whatever constituent an organization wants to reach must be the ultimate beneficiary of the partnerships created.

Much has been written in business literature about partnership, which tends to be defined along the lines of a legal relationship between two or more parties as part of a contractual arrangement.

The concept of a best partner, however, goes far beyond a legal relationship—just as marriage is more than two people whose names are affixed on a marriage license. A best partnership requires a holistic approach in which parties create win–win relationships across the value chain, from idea origination to product development to the customer's use of the product or service.

With a best partnership, an understanding exists: All parties know what the other is trying to accomplish now and in the future. This differs from a transaction that is focused largely on price—one party is trying to get the most out of the other, in a dynamic that is usually characterized as win–lose. This is not the case with best partnerships, which are no less competitive. However, they can be beneficial to all parties with a win–win scenario that stresses the benefit of a long-term arrangement.

In her book, *The Truth about Negotiations*, Professor Leigh Thompson of Northwestern University's Kellogg School of Management discusses how partners or potential partners often fight over issues without first understanding how they can create a win–win scenario. She illustrates this highly important concept using the well-known hypothetical scenario of two people fighting over an orange. Unable to resolve their positions that they both want and need the entire orange, they decided to cut it in half. However, had they taken the time to understand that one party wanted the juice and the other the zest (grated rind), they would have found a far better solution that would have given both of them exactly what they needed.[1]

As you can see, best partnerships require phenomenal communication skills, with the understanding that an enormous part of communicating is being a great listener. When open communication is established, then the only reason a party does not know something that would help the enterprise is: (1) one party did not ask or (2) another party did not share the information because it

---

[1] Leigh Thompson, *The Truth about Negotiations*, 2nd ed. (Upper Saddle River, NJ: FT Press, 2013).

assumed that everyone already knew. Communication drives a values-based partnership. When one party is willing to listen to find out what another wants or needs, then a true relationship can develop. Unlike adversarial parties in a competitive transaction, in a best partnership, the welfare of a partner entity is just as important as that of your own organization. The success of all parties is of common, long-term interest.

A best partnership, however, is still a business relationship. In Section Four we will discuss "best investments," so we are reminded that organizations have a fiduciary responsibility to generate a return for their owners. (Even not-for-profits must be financially sound and demonstrate to stakeholders that they are good stewards of resources.) A best partnership, therefore, must make sense from a business standpoint. Let's take the example of Baxter International, a health-care company that makes intravenous-drug delivery products. The company must purchase plastic resins from suppliers in order to make intravenous fluid bags. Rather than focusing solely on the price per pound, a best-partner conversation would take into consideration the issues that are most important to all involved: for example quantity, level of inventory, shipping costs, payment terms, and so forth. In fact, the company may be willing to pay a higher price per pound to secure a stable, consistent supply, while still realizing a net savings because the supplier agrees to maintain ideal inventory levels or accept extended payment terms.

In short, a best partnership does not last for merely one transaction. Rather, it is a strategic, long-term arrangement that pursues mutual ways in which both parties can be extremely successful.

In this section, we will look at best partnership from two distinct viewpoints. The first is using best partnerships with suppliers in a way that improves quality, enhances efficiency, fosters innovation, and creates positive experiences for the consumer. Our example here is NorthShore University HealthSystem, which has engaged strategically with best partners across its business landscape, from physician practices to a provider of health information technology (health IT). Because of the strength of its best partnerships, NorthShore has become a $2 billion integrated health-care system that has been rated one of the top 100 health-care systems in 16 of the last 19 years.[2]

The second example is when best partnerships become integrated to the point that a merger or acquisition occurs. What had been a best partner, either as an external supplier or even a customer, can be acquired and integrated into the organization, becoming part of its best team (showing how interrelated best team and best partner are, one building upon and contributing to the other). When a best partner is acquired, the integration risk is lower than in a typical acquisition. A high level of communication and understanding already exists among the parties in a best partnership, laying the groundwork for successful integration. Our example in Chapter 6 is Catamaran Corporation, a cutting-edge pharmacy benefits manager that successfully used a best-partner approach to grow the company both organically and through acquisitions, from $50 million in annual revenues to more than $20 billion in less than 10 years.

As we will see, by focusing on mutual successes, best partners heighten performance, improve the value proposition, and differentiate products or services in the marketplace. In the process, they may even transform industries through the creation of powerful new paradigms of partnership and competitiveness.

[2] Evanston Roundtable, "NorthShore University HealthSystem Named in Top 100 Hospitals for Record 16th Time," February 27, 2013, www.evanstonroundtable .com/main.asp?SectionID=4&SubSectionID=4&ArticleID=6829.

CHAPTER 5

SUPPLIERS AS BEST PARTNERS: A HOLISTIC RELATIONSHIP

When a best partnership exists, all are guided by a spirit of collaboration and mutual respect, instead of trying to squeeze every dime out of every business transaction. That's not to say that these relationships sacrifice the partners' ability to compete. In fact, they can reap a significant competitive advantage and, ultimately, more profitability by working together to satisfy customers and grow their businesses in a highly competitive environment. In this way, best partnerships are holistic and strategic.

As discussed in the introduction to Section Three, the need to create a best partnership stems from self-reflection on the part of the leader and his/her team as to the organization's value proposition. To simplify things, we might consider the example of the very early days of a start-up, with two or three people who have come together around a great new idea. As a team, they need to decide what they are really good at—where they can add the most value in the marketplace. That competitive advantage will be the core of the enterprise. Maybe this new entity has an advantage in how a product is engineered or how it is distributed. Whatever that distinction is, the team is absolutely passionate about it as the driver of the organization's economic engine.

As soon as the team has identified where the organization can create the most value, it needs to look externally toward creating partnerships that complete the picture. These partners (e.g., suppliers, manufacturers, distributors, etc.) are as passionate about the value they create as the organization itself. Everyone inside the company (best team) and among outside suppliers (best partners) recognizes that a holistic approach is necessary to create the kind of value that attracts and retains customers.

As discussed in Chapter 2, you need true self-confidence to identify what the organization is really good at, and it takes genuine humility to admit that it can't do everything. However, some executives and organizations refuse to concede that not everything can be done well internally; it hurts their egos. And even if your organization has the capability to do everything, that doesn't make it optimal. There are usually aspects of the business process that are best handled by others, which requires long-term, strategic best partnerships.

In a dynamic, fast-paced global marketplace, organizations must look for best partners to gain and keep their competitive advantage. Often, these relationships offer the end user tremendous added value that couldn't be provided by one company alone. In fact, the ideal way to think about the establishment of best partnerships is to look at it from the perspective of the client. Whatever the customer needs (e.g., quality, price, functionality, design, etc.), the partnership strives to deliver, with each party doing its best to offer solutions. Success is measured in satisfied customers and repeat business that should lead to greater profitability for all involved. This customer orientation also enhances accountability. In order to be best partners, each entity must be passionate about what it does to create value and enhance the seamless delivery of a product or service to the final customer. Every partner brings its best to the table, resulting in a value proposition in which one plus one equals three.

PARTNERSHIPS TO RESPOND TO COMPETITIVE PRESSURES

Organizations constantly face shifts and upheavals in the economic landscape. The market changes, technology evolves, new competitors come on the scene. Suddenly, the organization's model is no longer competitive. The company may decide to cut costs, which leads to the re-examination of every contract with suppliers of materials, components, and services. If the organization is big enough, it can pressure its suppliers, forcing them to agree to price cuts or longer payment terms. This is a classic win–lose scenario, in which the client organization has to get something out of the other parties in order to improve its competitive advantage.

All too often, however, this tactic fails because the client organization cannot find its way back to solid footing. That's not to say a company shouldn't review its supplier agreements to ensure that it's paying a fair price for what it is receiving. It absolutely should, but cost cutting as a way to improve the company often results in an adversarial relationship with suppliers, who are no longer motivated to work to create lasting, holistic value.

The alternative scenario is to have ongoing communication with suppliers and other best partners. Long before the competitive landscape changes, all parties are in close communication about what they see, including the emerging trends in the marketplace and their probable impact on the organization's ability to serve its customers. Even before it enters a difficult period, the organization is already talking with its partners about what needs to change in terms of supplies, quantities, pricing (which is but one of many considerations), specifications, or addressing the environmental and social impact of sourcing. In addition, best partners such as distributors could be part of an organization's "early warning system." In industries where the distributors are closer to the ultimate consumer, these partners are in a position to provide market intelligence that can help an organization stay ahead of the curve. For example, a best-partner distributor may inform the organization about changes in the type of packaging preferred by some customers (e.g., more environmentally friendly containers). Now the organization knows that if it does not switch its packaging, it could suffer serious market-share decline. In many cases, by working closely with its partners, the organization can determine how to address a situation before it escalates into a crisis.

In the midst of competitive pressures, it may be that the organization needs to lower its cost structure. However, instead of the organization demanding, say, a 20 percent discount from its suppliers, the parties are already in close communication. With a long-term commitment to work together, these best partners are more apt to come up with a solution (which may involve lower prices) that helps ensure the future viability of all involved, as we will see with the partnerships created by NorthShore University HealthSystem, which took a best-partner approach to health care.

LONG-TERM PARTNERSHIPS ARE EARNED

Not every supplier, distributor, or vendor will achieve the best-partner status that involves a long-term relationship with your organization. Over time, organizations may change partners. What had seemed like an appropriate fit later proves not to be ideal. In some cases, changes within one partner organization (e.g., new leadership, a shift in strategic direction, or acquisition or merger) may alter the trajectory. What had once been a close fit begins to diverge. In other cases, there may be deterioration in product quality or consistency of service. Whatever the reason, a supplier either loses its partnership status, or it never becomes a *best* partner in the first place.

The evolution from a single transaction or contract to a longer-term relationship is typically a process that is tested and proven over time. This is not only the case with the supplier, but also the organization, itself. Both parties have to prove their best-partner fit with the willingness and capability of advancing the goals of all parties in a win–win scenario.

Discernment in forming best partnerships is crucial. When an organization is successful, it will find that many parties want to be its strategic partners. Yet, true partnership is demonstrated with consistent execution, proven values, and cultural fit between two parties. Close alignment is paramount when a partner has customer contact. In order for an organization to allow another party to have access to its customers, whether they are individuals or other businesses, it must be assured of how that partner acts in the marketplace.

In fact, the best way to think about the establishment of a best partnership is to view it from the customer perspective. What will the impact be on the end user? Will the consumer experience be enhanced in some meaningful way because of this partnership—perhaps by greater efficiency, improved quality, enhanced consistency, or other benefits? If the partnership does not improve the end user's perception or experience, then it does not serve the organization. In order for a partner to earn the title of *best*, it must make a measurable difference to the organization in the most demanding of all proving grounds—the marketplace—with the seamless delivery of products or services to consumers.

The analogy for a long-term best partnership is a successful marriage. Having been married for 35 years, I do have a perspective on relationships that, in private one-on-one conversations, I'm sometimes asked to share with students. For example, one of my students told me that he and his girlfriend had been dating for some time and were ready to contemplate the next step. "How do I know if I've found the right life partner?" the student asked me. "We've been together for awhile now, and I want to know if this is the right person to share the rest of my life with."

The emotional depth and honesty of his question touched me, and I was flattered that this student would come to me for my opinion. Based on my experience, I shared with him that one way of determining whether someone is *the one* is to think about the importance of her happiness or fulfillment. As I explained to the student, if making his girlfriend happy is so important that it even eclipses his own fulfillment, then that speaks volumes about the kind of relationship that they have. At the same time, a healthy relationship is not about being a selfless martyr. His girlfriend, too, must be just as focused on *his* happiness. When each party is committed to the other's well-being, growth, fulfillment, and joy, then a true partnership exists, which becomes a great foundation for a marriage. In other words, for a relationship to last over the long term, there must be give and take by both parties, which sets up a win–win scenario. Any sacrifices entailed—for example, he doesn't take a job in San Francisco so that they can stay together in Chicago while she finishes her graduate degree—do not really involve giving up anything substantial, because over the long term both parties are fulfilled through the relationship and their willingness to give to each other.

This highly personal example gets to the heart of what a best partnership is all about, even as it applies in a business context. Best partners who work together over the long-term are equally committed to each other's success. There may be sacrifices by one party or another, but together they will attain a higher level of achievement than if they had operated independently or stayed at the transactional level. Mutual commitment to one another is really what being the best is all about: laying the foundation of trust, mutual respect, and long-term collaboration that truly makes a difference for all parties.

NORTHSHORE UNIVERSITY HEALTHSYSTEM: COLLABORATION IN ACTION

One industry that has been dramatically impacted by changes in the regulatory and competitive landscape is health care. Among the pressures being felt by health-care organizations today are the need for greater efficiency, increased use of health information technology (health IT), and improvements in quality, patient safety, and satisfaction. For one health system in particular, North-Shore University HealthSystem, based in Evanston, Illinois, taking a best-partner approach has enabled it to pursue excellence holisti-cally as a values-based organization. Today, NorthShore consists of four hospitals in the Chicago area, medical group offices covering more than 900 primary care physicians and specialists, laboratory services, and pharmacies. On top of that, NorthShore and Advo-cate Health Care have announced a plan to combine, creating Advocate NorthShore Health Partners, which would be the largest integrated health care delivery system in Illinois and the 11th largest not-for-profit health care system in the United States. (The merger is subject to regulatory approval.)

Like a successful organization in any industry, NorthShore takes a strategic, long-term approach to its best partnerships in order to optimize win–win arrangements for all parties.

"Developing long-term relationships still matters, even in a world that's largely driven by transactions,"[1] says Mark R. Neaman, who has served as president and CEO of NorthShore University Health-System since 1992. Mark is widely recognized as a leader in the health-care industry and has been honored with a number of distinctions, including the prestigious Gold Medal Award from the American College of Healthcare Executives in 2009 and being named Healthcare CEO of the Year by HIMSS/Modern Healthcare.

"In an industry such as ours, you've got to think long-term because of the time and cost involved," Mark adds. "It is less costly to do business with someone who is a long-term partner, instead of continuously redoing transactions."

Pursuing long-term relationships with partners also promotes consistency, particularly in the experience of the consumer or end

[1] Mark R. Neaman, telephone interview, July 11, 2014. Quotes and data regarding NorthShore University HealthSystem come from this interview unless a footnote indicates otherwise.

user. For NorthShore, its best partnerships have led directly to consistent performance at a high level, earning the organization a rating as one of the top 100 hospitals in 16 of the last 19 years.[2] "An organization may have high points followed by low points," Mark says. "We're targeting, year after year, consistent performance."

Among the strategic, best partnerships that NorthShore has put in place, one of the most compelling is in health IT, particularly electronic medical records (EMRs, also known as electronic health records). EMRs are considered superior to paper records because they contribute to improvements in patient care by increasing the accuracy of diagnoses and health outcomes, facilitating care coordination, and increasing efficiencies, cost savings, and patient participation in care.[3]

More than a dozen years ago, NorthShore made the decision to implement a comprehensive health IT system, and today is recognized for having one of the leading EMR programs in the country. This would not have been possible without a strategic best partner: Epic Systems Corporation, a Wisconsin-based company that specializes in health IT systems for large and mid-size health-care organizations. "An EMR system is one of those classic examples of something you could technically do by yourself, if you recruit the right people and have the resources. Or, you could partner with someone," Mark explains.

Going back to the first premise of forming best partnerships, NorthShore decided that its strengths were in providing excellent patient care. Partnering with a third party that had the same level of commitment to health IT would lead to further differentiation in the marketplace. Thus, the NorthShore–Epic Systems collaboration is a perfect example of the "one plus one equals three" power of best partners. Bringing together parties that have significant strengths in

[2] Evanston Roundtable, "NorthShore University HealthSystem Named in Top 100 Hospitals for Record 16th Time," February 27, 2013. www.evanstonroundtable.com/ main.asp?SectionID=4&SubSectionID=4&ArticleID=6829.

[3] HealthIT.gov, "Benefits of Electronic Health Records," 2014. www.healthit .gov/providers-professionals/benefits-electronic-health-records-ehrs.

complementary areas creates an entity that is far greater than any of them would be alone. Moreover, these best partners bring to the table the value created by their own best-team environments in service of a bigger mission or purpose. For NorthShore and Epic Systems, their best partnership resulted in an exemplary model of EMR in action to promote better patient outcomes, higher satisfaction, and clinical excellence.

As with any best partnership, the NorthShore–Epic Systems combination was not without risk. For one thing, Epic Systems was not the largest player in this space and had not implemented EMR in a hospital environment. At the time, all health IT systems had their share of bugs to be worked out. (A major crash at a large, prestigious hospital alerted the industry to how much a faulty IT system can disrupt operations.) "We were looking at ourselves and asking, 'Are we sure we want to do this?' But we felt it was important to transform the organization by working with a partner that could develop the software we needed," Mark explains.

Because of Epic Systems' responsiveness and willingness to create an EMR solution tailored to NorthShore's needs, it quickly emerged as a best partner in this health IT undertaking. Implementation of EMR at NorthShore, however, could only be successful if it was embraced throughout the organization. In simpler terms: Technology can be a potent tool, but it can only be effective if it is widely used. Once again, we find the intersection between best partner and best team. Within an organization, a best-team mindset means creating and reinforcing the internal culture to accept and adopt the contribution of the best partner, whether a technological tool or a particular service. Otherwise, the collaboration will not be seamless and, therefore, will never reach the full potential of a best partnership. For NorthShore, that meant doctors, nurses, and other clinicians needed to adopt and embrace EMR.

"We made a cultural commitment to say, 'We are going to do this and we're going to do this right. Using EMR is going to be the NorthShore way,'" Mark recalls.

A strong selling point for NorthShore's internal best team was the potential for EMR to reduce errors, improve patient safety and outcomes, and reduce time wasted trying to get information (for example, a complete record of a patient's medications). "We got 95 percent of the people bought in. They enthusiastically embraced it," Mark says.

Buy-in was supported through a rollout that included in-depth education for all team members, with ongoing communication as well as technical training. People felt supported through the process of implementation, which further encouraged adoption, while also addressing issues and questions as they arose. The success of the EMR roll-out is evidenced by an impressive statistic: Full implementation, which often takes as long as five years, was accomplished at NorthShore in only 15 months.

The EMR rollout was so successful, in fact, that NorthShore became a demonstration site for Epic Systems, with hundreds of health-care organizations coming to Evanston to view health IT in action. NorthShore made this commitment because it was part of the win–win scenario. The demonstrations helped Epic Systems reach other potential clients, which benefited the growth of its business; while NorthShore could also help with the development of next-generation products that would meet their specific needs, which was in its best interest. In addition, as a demonstration site for EMR, NorthShore's reputation in the healthcare industry was enhanced.

BUILDING PARTNERSHIPS ON PARTNERSHIPS

Most organizations will have more than one strategic partnership. A manufacturer, for example, could have best partners across its supply chain, from sourcing to distribution. This adds complexity to the system, as partners must not only work with the organization but also with each other to achieve overarching goals such as enhanced quality, greater efficiency, and customer satisfaction.

If independent entities only see their part of the project, it will be difficult to achieve seamless integration.

Consider the example of Boeing's 787 Dreamliner, which is manufactured largely from outsourced components, while the aircraft company assumes the role of assembler. These sophisticated aircraft, which have taken years longer to build than originally proposed, are highly complex with demanding specifications that require unprecedented engineering. The rear body of the plane is composed of about 6,000 parts, many of which had to be created from scratch. According to MIT's Innovation@work blog, early on, many of those components failed to meet Boeing's requirements, increasing costs and creating delays. When the first Dreamliner arrived at the assembly plant, there were 30,000 pieces to work with—a huge difference from the 1,200 parts the original designs were based on. On top of that, thousands of parts were missing.[4] These problems could possibly have been reduced with better communication among the partners.

Granted, most organizations are not faced with the complexity of building a large commercial aircraft from independently manufactured components. Nonetheless, the success of a partnership can be *make or break* for an organization as it tries to improve its operations, to recover from a weaker position or gain a competitive advantage. Often, such endeavors involve building partnerships on top of partnerships, layering one initiative over another.

In the case of NorthShore University HealthSystem, its EMR rollout with Epic Systems was layered on top of another best partnership with its physicians. Currently, NorthShore's faculty practice plan consists of more than 900 physicians who are employees, fully integrated within the system. In addition, NorthShore has relationships with more than 500 independent physicians and

[4]MIT Sloan Executive Education, "Will Risk Result in Reward for Boeing's Dreamliner?" July 2013. http://executive.mit.edu/blog/2013/07/boeing-outsourcing-vertical-integration/.

specialists who are not at the hospital on a daily basis, but who may see patients on site from time to time.

The physician best partnership is based on what Mark calls the "Mayo Clinic model," as a nod to the organization that pioneered this strategy. The Mayo Clinic model, which NorthShore adopted in 1992, is a tightly integrated delivery system that combines the resources of the hospital with primary care and specialty physicians. Here, too, we find the intersection between best partner and best team. Where an affiliation exists with an independent physician practice, the dynamic is one of best partners who work together to achieve the common goal of excellence in health-care delivery. When those physician practices are acquired, the doctors become part of NorthShore's internal best team. NorthShore has acquired a significant number of physician groups—approximately 40 in the past four years. Most of these practices are relatively small, consisting of three to five physicians per group. For the physicians, being acquired by a strong partner such as NorthShore is attractive given the increasing difficulty for physician groups to thrive in today's regulatory environment with the financial pressures associated with managed care.

As a best partner and best team, the physician integration model allows for greater collaboration across the health system, enabling primary care doctors and specialists to work closely together to provide comprehensive care to patients. "Medicine is so complex. You've got to make sure primary care physicians are inter-relating with specialists. But you can't forget about the pathologists and the lab. All parties have to be working on behalf of the patient," Mark said. "By partnering with physicians, the health system is able to bring together all parties."

For NorthShore's patients (their ultimate end users) a best partnership between the hospital and the physicians allows for comprehensive, holistic treatment. NorthShore doctors treat not only the specific health episode that triggered hospitalization, but they also address other conditions that impact the individual's health and wellness. Here, the EMR system put in place by Epic Systems adds an important dimension to the physician partnership. As primary care doctors, specialists, nurses, and other clinicians collaborate in treatment, the EMR allows them all full access to the patient's relevant health information, from previous hospitalizations and treatments to current medications. The result is a holistic approach that creates the best possible outcome for the patient.

Taking a best-partner approach also shifts thinking in terms of an individual doctor to realizing the multiplier effect of a larger team. To illustrate, Mark gives an example. Family members and friends facing particular health issues often ask him who is the best doctor to treat them. "I tell them that's the wrong question," he says. "They should be asking what the best health system is to treat them. What they need is not just one doctor, but a team of physicians and caregivers, along with a health system that has all the information about that person to make it work."

Moreover, a team approach enables a comprehensive response to a patient's health issue, from making the correct diagnosis to putting together a care plan and treatment regimen to meet the patient's needs. "You can't do that unless you've created a partnership with all the right relationships in place," Mark adds.

SUCCESS BUILDS ON SUCCESS

As partnerships are layered on partnerships (e.g., NorthShore's EMR initiative with its physician network) the benefits are compounded. The positive results achieved by these partnerships generate enthusiasm that attracts other parties that also want to become best partners, because they see the upside of being in a strategic relationship with the organization. Thus, a virtuous cycle is created.

For example, NorthShore has partnered with the University of Chicago Pritzker School of Medicine to further their mutual goals of medical education, clinical investigation, and excellence in patient care. This best partnership combines the unique strengths of both organizations in a win–win arrangement. NorthShore benefits from having access to the Pritzker School's medical research and cutting-edge programs, especially those in areas such as complex care and biomedical science. Having access to research-level tools and treatments helps to attract patients as well as physicians. "The benefits to us include the research environment and the prestige factor, which helps us to attract physician talent and gain access to research grants," Mark says.

For the Pritzker School, best-partner NorthShore provides a clinical setting in which to train its residents and medical students and to conduct medical research. For example, through North-Shore, the university is able to tap a large patient base for clinical trials—a capability that is further enhanced by the Epic Systems EMR that can be used to identify eligible patients. As Mark observes, "Success builds upon success."

Other partnerships within the health system cover materials management, such as NorthShore's 20-year relationship with Cardinal Health, whose services include inventory management of pharmaceuticals and other healthcare supplies. Such long-term best partnerships are built on trust and respect for each party's expertise.

The criticism, Mark acknowledged, is that with a long-term partnership, an organization may not always be getting the *best deal* in terms of pricing on every single product or service. "In some respects, that's probably true," he added. "Therefore, there has to be some balance in the process—some pressure testing" to make sure pricing and terms remain competitive and in keeping with the win–win philosophy of benefit to both parties (e.g., competitive, fair prices for the organization and the guarantee of long-term volume for the supplier).

Having a long-term relationship, however, ultimately saves time and money by avoiding the need to bid out each and every product or service. Moreover, a transactional model cannot create a best partnership that leads to the kind of seamless integration that takes an organization to the next level in terms of innovation, creative solutions, quality, and continuous improvement. Only when best partners are literally invested in each other's success can such synergies be fully optimized. "Long-term partners are 'all in' and that helps everyone," Mark says.

For the organization and its best partners, the scope of view expands from a single product or service, needed at a specific point in time, to the whole picture across the continuum of current needs and future opportunities.

BEST PARTNERS AND THE PURSUIT OF EXCELLENCE

Whether it's a start-up or an existing enterprise with a long track record, an organization soon learns that it cannot go it alone. At some point, even a vertically integrated company requires strategic partners for supplies or services that it cannot produce or deliver on its own. Identifying where the enterprise needs to partner with others starts with self-reflection on the organizational level: What does the organization do well to create value, and what aspects of its operation or process are better served by other entities that have specific strengths in those areas? Rather than being linked to a single transaction—a price-driven purchase—a best partnership evolves over time, giving each party time to appreciate what the others bring to the table.

Best partnerships, by definition, are win–win propositions. They do not exist only for the benefit of the organization alone or its supplier or distributor. Rather, the partnership benefits all parties involved, especially the customer whose experience is enhanced in a meaningful way.

CHAPTER 6

BUILDING BEST-PARTNER CUSTOMER RELATIONSHIPS

O rganizations have two types of customers. The first is the customer that has a transactional relationship with the company, centered mostly on the price. The second is the customer that is a true partner. Although both types of customers are buying products and services, when there is a best partnership between the company and its customers, the benefits spread across the entire value chain.

To complete our discussion of best partnerships, we explore the dynamic of a best partnership between customer and company. In Chapter 5, we examined the best partnerships that occur *upstream*, between a company and its suppliers. Now, we move *downstream* to explore the benefits of having a partnership between a company and its customer, such that the success of one is intimately tied to the success of the other. A best partnership becomes a connection that brings the parties into closer coordination on the development, supply, and delivery of products and services in the marketplace.

The obvious bias of my background aside, I believe health care is one of the most dramatic examples of how a supplier–customer best partnership can bring a significant benefit to the end user— the patient. During my time at Baxter International, when I was a division president and later CFO, president, and eventually CEO, I witnessed how our customers valued the partnerships that were created around the critically important medical products that, without exaggeration, made a life-or-death difference in the lives of patients. Today, as an executive partner at Madison Dearborn Partners, I work closely with the health-care companies in our portfolio and study all aspects of the industry. In addition, I serve on the boards of several healthcare companies and hospitals. I see tremendous benefits that customer best partnerships offer to increase cost-effectiveness and efficiency in health care. Later in this chapter, we will look at the example of Catamaran Corporation, a pharmacy benefit manager (PBM) and one of the fastest growing companies in *any* industry.

WHAT A CUSTOMER BEST PARTNERSHIP IS—AND ISN'T

Building customer relationships is certainly nothing new, given the intense focus for roughly the past two decades on customer relationship management (CRM). Used largely as a sales tool, as well as for customer service and support, CRM is meant to track customer needs, the frequency of customer contact, responsiveness to specific campaigns, and so forth. While CRM can lead to better effectiveness in sales and customer service and support functions, it does not, by itself, lead to partnership. That takes in-depth understanding and a deeper level of commitment and collaboration.

In addition, much has been written about customer satisfaction—the thought that a happy, satisfied customer is more likely to be a loyal purchaser as well. Customer-building initiatives, *when implemented well* (a key point!), can make a difference compared to a purely commercial standpoint, as greater customer loyalty translates into higher sales. However, this does not automatically constitute a best partnership. Partnership is a win–win that benefits both parties, in pursuit of the specific goals of each.

We're reminded of the importance of *balance and perspective*, one of the four principles of values-based leadership. Companies clearly want to serve their customers, but this can only be done reasonably and sustainably with balance. To use a simplified example, if a company cut the price of its products or services by 50 percent, its customers would undoubtedly be very happy. But if the company goes out of business because of a significant decline in profitability, that price cut would hardly be an effective customer-satisfaction strategy, let alone a best partnership. Not only is the company bankrupt, but its customers have also lost an important supplier!

The old adage that *the customer is always right* also has its limitations and drawbacks. The customer is important, and the customer does come first. But that does not mean that the customer is right on every issue. With a best partnership, a relationship exists in which the customer feels important and valued, without needing to always be *right* (which often implies that the supplier is *wrong*). A far better way to think about best-partner customer relationships is whether the arrangement is so important, so satisfying, that the customer would recommend the supplier to others. This speaks volumes about the benefit of the partnership.

With a best partnership, both parties truly understand each other and what matters most to the customer and the company. Customers see their suppliers as being vital to their current and future success, to the point that they do not believe they can be successful without the company's involvement. This kind of partnership is only possible when both parties move beyond the transaction to focus on the *value chain*.

FOCUS ON THE VALUE CHAIN

With a best-partner approach, the supplier and customer engage in broader and deeper dialogue that encompasses the entire value chain. For example, in the case of Baxter, rather than focusing only on the price of the product, we sought to understand the total cost structure for hospitals that purchased products from us. This included the cost of storing the product in a warehouse, the cost of transporting the product from a distribution center to the hospital, and so forth. As a result, we could enter into best-partner relationships with our customers, in which we delivered products *just in time*—not only to their distribution centers, but also to the particular floor or unit of the hospital on a *just-as-needed* basis. This entire process became known as the Baxter Value Link Program.

The ultimate best-partnerships resulted in customers no longer needing a distribution center (thereby eliminating that cost), because they had built up enough trust in us as their supplier. Think about it: These hospitals had the confidence that the supplies they needed to perform an operation—sometimes a life-or-death situation—would be there when we said it would be. These best partnerships did not occur automatically, but rather were the results of in-depth discussions with our customers, and the time we took to understand global logistics, usage patterns, and optimal inventory levels. Price was only one part of the total value equation.

Another example is that, years ago, a medical products company such as Baxter could provide 15 or 20 different supplies to the hospital, which hospital staff would have to gather into bundles in advance of specific procedures. Before an open heart surgery or a hip replacement, for example, the hospital staff would take the time to gather the sterile instruments and supplies needed for that operation (e.g., scalpel, scissors, retractors, sutures, gauze, tape, etc.).

Many years ago, Baxter saw the opportunity to deepen its customer relationships with a new line called Custom Sterile, which provided sterile supply packs customized for specific operations or procedures. The cost savings in terms of storage and time was significant, and the product line contributed to greater efficiency in the operating room, which is the most expensive area of the hospital. Buying sterile pre-packaged instruments and supplies enabled hospitals to perform more surgeries in a day, thus increasing their revenues and, more important, providing more patients with the treatment they needed on a timely basis.

THE HUMAN ELEMENT

On the surface, a supply chain is about the movement of goods and services from manufacturer to distributor to end user. It involves such unemotional elements as cost of goods and logistics. Going deeper, however, the picture changes when questions arise such as: Who are the end users? What is behind the demand and urgency for obtaining these products and services? What would be the consequences of supply disruption? In short, what is the impact of this product or service on the lives of the ultimate end users—the patients and their families? The answers to these questions provide context and meaning to the supply chain, and remind all parties why the partnership is far more than a mere transaction.

All businesses and industries have their human elements. Consider traffic safety equipment and software that keep people safe on the highways and reduce accidents and, therefore, injuries and fatalities. Think about the food industry and the importance of safety, quality, and nutrition for millions of consumers. With this perspective, a company making a circuit or a shut-off switch isn't just supplying some small component in a much bigger part—*widgets* rolling off an assembly line—it is helping to ensure quality and safety for consumers who purchase all types of products from home electronics to power generation to automobiles. This way of thinking can make things real and meaningful across the organization, from senior management to team members in sales, product development, customer support, and production.

One of the most dramatic examples from my own experience involves Edwards Lifesciences Corporation, which makes and markets heart valves and related repair products. Edwards was one of Baxter's most successful businesses, and today it is an independent, publicly traded company. To connect a product line with a human face, the company invites patients who received an Edwards heart valve to the manufacturing plant. It is always an emotional moment when a patient stands on the floor of the production facility and says, "Thank you for all you do. If you hadn't made my heart valve, I wouldn't be here to thank you."

Visits by patients to the production plant floor forged an emotional connection that went far beyond the supply chain. Edwards employees did not look at hospitals or group purchasing organizations (GPOs) as their customers. Rather, those entities were partners with Edwards in providing the heart valves that were vital to the health and longevity of the final customers—people with names and faces.

In any business or industry, making the human connection, whenever possible, adds purpose and passion to the partnership, aligning even more closely the supplier with customer, for the benefit of the ultimate end user.

GROWING THE BUSINESS WITH BEST PARTNERSHIPS: CATAMARAN CORPORATION

One of the most impressive success stories in any industry is Catamaran Corporation, which has grown in revenue from $50 million in 2006 to $20 billion in 2014. Along the way, Catamaran defined a client-centered business model as a pharmacy benefit manager (PBM), with offerings that are customized based on the needs of the health benefit payers (insurers and employers) and their members. Its chairman and CEO is Mark Thierer, who has more than 30 years of health-care experience.

Today, Catamaran is a leading provider of PBM services, as well as health IT solutions. Its offerings are aimed at lowering the cost and reducing the complexity of prescription drug programs across the pharmaceutical supply chain, from retail and mail-order pharmacies to health-care plans and managed care organizations. It also owns and operates a network of mail-order and specialty pharmacies.

In his 2013 letter to shareholders, Mark highlighted the advancements in the health-care arena and their impact on the pharmacy business, "from development of new therapies to emerging technologies and use of big data and prescriptive analytics." He highlighted promising developments for the future, including "highly personalized therapies, interactions, and interventions [for patients]." For providers, he touched on more holistic ways to view their patients' information to provide "more effective diagnosis and prescribing, and new ways to . . . collaborate in real time." Finally, for payers Mark mentioned "new opportunities for population management based on a mix of prescriptive data modeling and real-time interventions."[1]

The breadth of the Catamaran product line today is the result of strategic growth, both organically and through acquisitions. At every stage of its evolution, Catamaran maintained a best-partner approach that aligned with some of the biggest players in the pharmaceutical supply chain—even to the point of acquiring and merging with some of them.

The Catamaran story begins with a predecessor company, SXC Health Solutions, which Mark joined in 2006 as a board member. After attending only three quarterly board meetings, Mark was asked to become part of the company's leadership team in September of 2006, first as president and chief operating officer, and later as chairman and CEO.[2]

When Mark joined SXC it was a $50 million, pure technology player, providing software products that processed pharmacy claims and delivered clinical functionality for health plans and other payers. Over the years, through a strategic expansion of its business to become a full-service PBM, SXC experienced a

---

[1] Mark Thierer, "Letter to Shareholders," Catamaran Corporation 2013 Annual Report, 2014.
[2] Mark Thierer, telephone interview, July 14, 2014. Quotes and information regarding Catamaran come from this interview unless a footnote indicates otherwise.

compound annual growth rate of 50 percent and a 50-fold increase in shareholder value. In 2011, *Fortune* named SXC the number-one fastest growing company in the United States. In 2012, SXC merged with Catalyst Health Solutions to create Catamaran.

The growth and transformation of the business, first as SXC and then as Catamaran, is grounded in the belief that best partnerships provide a context for holistic solutions to be developed and delivered within the supply chain for the ultimate benefit of the end user. "I believe that strong client relationships and strong trading partner relationships are worth their weight in gold," Mark says.

This view, he explained, was formed early Mark's career, when he was with IBM and responsible for its health-industry sales management. Later, he held positions at companies such as Caremark Rx, which is now part of CVS Caremark, a PBM and specialty pharmacy company. In every position he held, Mark saw the importance of building strong customer relationships for the long term, based on in-depth knowledge of the customer's business. "You need to be an expert in the client's or trading partner's business, with an intimate understanding of its P&L [profit and loss] statement. That means becoming totally invested in those client relationships," he says. "I've often said that these business relationships are like a good marriage. If you commit to fixing and improving the relationship on an ongoing basis, it can become much stronger over time."

Mark describes Catamaran's business as helping to organize the supply chain, from pharmaceutical manufacturer, to wholesalers, to retail drug distribution. As a PBM, it delivers clinically relevant cost-containment solutions for pharmaceuticals, biotech medications, and generic drugs that are ultimately used by consumers. It also serves pharmacy and retail chain partners, including drug stores, big-box stores, and grocery stores that have pharmacy departments.

A snapshot of Catamaran's business model reveals a robust stream of products and services, aligning payers, providers, and patients. As a PBM, Catamaran gets paid every time a prescription is filled. Its services, however, are more comprehensive than just enabling the dispensing of prescription drugs. It is on the frontline of helping customers manage health plan costs, the bulk of which are for physician or hospital visits (accounting for about 85 percent of all U.S. health-care spending). The value proposition for a PBM is to make sure health plans have the lowest cost medications, and that patients take them as prescribed to improve their health and avoid hospitalization and unnecessary doctor visits. "At the highest level, the notion of the best partner approach in the PBM space is very relevant. We're not making anything. Rather, we're creating value through partnering," Mark says.

While best-partnership thinking may be more intuitive with a supplier of a particular product or service and its customers, it applies to almost all organizations. A non-profit foundation, for example, can create best partnerships with donors (i.e., the *suppliers* of its funding) as well as recipients of grants or other services (i.e., its client base) by knowing how each defines value and success. On the one hand, a foundation might be able to create a closer best partnership with a particular donor based on mutual goals, such as a joint commitment to a certain mission, purpose, or project. On the other hand, a best partnership with grant recipients may lead to educational, cultural, or other enrichment activities that enhance the purpose of the foundation and its recipients. This best partnership also benefits the community at large and donors, who supply funding to realize a particular mission. The specifics of the best-partnership strategies will vary depending on the type and purpose of the organizations involved. Common to all is the desire to create and promote win–win scenarios that result in each party's success being directly tied to that of the others.

BEST PARTNERSHIPS PROMOTE INNOVATION

Another benefit of best partnership between suppliers and customers is the opportunity to promote innovation on both sides of the value chain—upstream to manufacturer or downstream to distributor or end user. Catamaran's organic growth stemmed from its innovation. As Mark took over operations of SXC, he saw the opportunity to transform the company from selling software to PBMs to becoming a PBM itself. He started with a best-team approach, identifying the specific skill sets he needed on his team. "I brought a set of strengths and a track record. I knew the leaders in sales and strategy," he says. "But I never pretended I was a financial engineer. I filled those gaps" by recruiting people with strengths in complementary areas that would bolster SXC's talent bench.

One such team member is Jeff Park, who joined SXC as executive vice president and CFO, after leaving Covington Capital Partners, a venture capital firm that had invested in SXC. Working together, Mark and Jeff guided the company through several significant milestones of growth, becoming a publicly traded firm on the Nasdaq, and then completing eight acquisitions. Other members recruited for the SXC best team were some of Mark's former colleagues from his Caremark days, "a core team that I lived with in the foxhole for between five and fifteen years of my life," he recalls. "It [recruiting these former colleagues] didn't go down without a little shrapnel, but we got it done. We brought in a core set of functional experts who possessed what we needed at this pivotal time of strategy change."

As Mark described in Chapter 4, he personally led the recruiting and hiring of the leadership team, something he continues to take pride in today. This is highly unusual for CEOs, many of whom may spend an hour or two with a finalist, but otherwise expect human resources and recruiters to do the bulk of the screening and hiring. Mark, however, believes that the best way to improve the success rate of hiring for the leadership team is to be intimately involved in the process.

In 2008, the transformation of SXC was complete. Mark remembers it as the year "we literally bet the company, as we went from a product company to a service company." Looking back, he credits the success of the transformation to being self-reflective, which allowed him to become his best self and create a best team that had the vision and courage to "recognize our goal and carry out our strategy" as the company evolved from software-only, to software and data-center services, and, finally, into a full-service PBM.

This business transformation, however, meant that SXC was entering the business that its customers already were in. And yet, SXC did so in a way that did not undermine those relationships. The secret? SXC retained a best-partner mindset. "We made an agreement that said, basically, we won't solicit your current clients. But in the open market, you're going to have to compete with us," Mark says. Obviously, the trust issue was huge. Information such as pricing and customer relationships had to be kept confidential—as Mark puts it "firewalled off, not just from competitors but also from ourselves in the PBM business."

By creating trusting best partnerships, SXC was then able to take the next step in its growth by making a series of successful acquisitions.

WHEN A BEST PARTNER BECOMES AN ACQUISITION

All enterprises, large or small, public or private, need to grow in order to thrive. Growth can be accomplished in two different ways. The first is organic, by growing the existing business, as a company makes and delivers more or expands its line of products and services. The second is by acquiring another company or business unit. An acquisition may involve a company in a different line of business. Or, it may be a natural extension of the business, such as to vertically integrate backward by acquiring a supplier, or forward by acquiring distributors or customers.

To some people, acquisitions seem to make so much sense— Company A plus Company B equals a much larger operation with more revenues, an expanded product line, greater market share, and so forth. To them, it seems to make so much sense to acquire growth rather than go through the pain and effort of trying to grow the business organically. My guess is that people who think this way don't have much experience with acquisitions.

Acquisitions are very challenging, from the due diligence through the negotiations and, most difficult of all, integration of two companies. Little wonder then, that, as studies have shown, some 80 percent of acquisitions never earn their cost of capital. In other words, in four out of five cases, regardless of the amount of money paid, the acquiring company would have been better off not doing the deal.

Of all the reasons why many acquisitions don't live up to expectations (which I define as being *failed* acquisitions) the one that gets talked about the most is when the acquiring company overpays. The root cause, however, may very well be that the acquirer became emotional. The leadership team starts to describe the acquisition in emotionally charged terms; they've *got* to have that business! If they need it so badly that they're willing to pay more than anyone else then, well, they can have it. If they define winning as paying more than anyone else would pay, then they win. But they end up losing because they overpaid, and their shareholders suffer the consequences.

Another reason why acquisitions fail is that people confuse the economics with strategy. I can recall having team members tell me that they wanted to make an acquisition, and when I asked why, they answered, "Because it's very strategic." Our discussion unfolded something like this:

Me: "Do the economics make sense?"
Team member: "Oh, it's very strategic."
Me: "Let's talk about the economics. How about the net present value, the amount of cash generated by the business?"
Team member: "Harry, this acquisition is so strategic, it's way beyond net present value."

That, to me, is a *very* scary place to be, since net present value takes into account the entire future of the business! Bottom line: An acquisition might appear to be strategic, but if the economics don't make sense, then by definition, it's not strategic. (A little self-reflection on the matter would make that point clear, as would balance and perspective to gather the opinions and viewpoints of others on the acquisition, the economics of it, and its strategic value.)

Now let's say that a potential acquisition does make sense from the standpoint of the numbers. The economics work, and strategically it looks promising. Do you go ahead and make the deal? Again, not so fast. In running the numbers and doing the calculations, no one has spent any time examining whether or not this acquisition would make any sense in terms of cultural fit. And if anything can derail an acquisition after the fact, it's a poor fit! A classic acquisition culture clash was the merger of Daimler-Benz with Chrysler in the late 1990s. As *The Economist* noted in 2000, "Cross-border mergers are notoriously tricky. For DaimlerChrysler to succeed requires cohesion not just between two headquarters, in Stuttgart and Auburn Hills, Michigan, but also between a host of offices and factories with different national and corporate cultures."[3] From a cultural-fit standpoint, the merger didn't work. In 2007, the nine-year, $36 billion matchup of Chrysler and Daimler-Benz ended in a $7.4 billion sale of Chrysler, resulting in more than $28 billion in lost shareholder value. Moral of the story: When cultures don't mesh, it doesn't matter how good the numbers look.

Using a simplified, hypothetical example, here's how things can go wrong: Let's say a company has a strong engineering mentality and is very focused on prioritization, process, and framework. Understanding the facts is a cultural value. Now, let's say that this company is looking at acquiring a firm with a sales and

[3] "The DaimlerChrysler Emulsion," *The Economist*, July 27 2000, www.economist .com/node/341352.

marketing culture. Would you expect that these two companies are going to find a way to work together successfully?

Once again, self-reflection is a valuable tool in the leadership toolbox. Through self-reflection, leaders can consider what their company is really good at, what its core values and strengths are, and how the leadership team operates. For the leader of the company with the engineering mentality, key questions to ponder would be: "Are we really going to be flexible enough and balanced enough, and have sufficient true self-confidence, to welcome the leaders of a company with a sales and marketing culture to join our management team? Do we have enough openness and genuine humility to accept them and their viewpoints?" If leaders do not self-reflect on these and related issues, then they'll be left to their assumptions—meaning they'll assume that somehow it will all work out. An assumption like that one is an invitation to disaster.

There can be many warning signs of impending disaster, if a leader is self-reflective enough to recognize them. Once I was a division president in the midst of making an acquisition, and the business we were looking at buying was in product areas that were different from what we did, but represented a logical extension. I asked our general manager how important it was to retain the management of the company we were acquiring. In other words, if senior management did not stay on after the acquisition, could we successfully operate the business?

The general manager told me that, yes, the senior managers were necessary; we couldn't successfully run the business without them. However, the general manager assured me that we shouldn't worry about that at all. These senior managers just loved our company and our culture, and they almost got emotional every time they talked about what a great fit this was going to be. Being a little more cynical and having been burned previously, I asked one simple question: "How much money would each of the senior managers take away from the transaction?"

Enter what I now refer to as "The Island Problem." We did the deal with the assumption that we had nothing to worry about regarding the senior management of the acquired company. They loved us and couldn't wait to come to work for us—or so we thought. On the fifth day after closing the acquisition, our management team called for a meeting with the senior managers of the acquired firm. Nobody showed up. Why? Well, my assumption is that they were on an island somewhere far away with all the money they'd made on the deal.

Moral of this story: know the company you're going to acquire—know them inside and out. Know the leaders, their motivations and desires, their values and cultures. In short, reduce your risk with a best-partner approach.

THE POSTER CHILD OF BEST-PARTNER DEALS

When SXC agreed to buy Catalyst Health Solutions in a $4.4 billion deal in April 2012 it knew exactly what it was getting. Catalyst had been a client of SXC for about 10 years. SXC provided the entire claims processing engine inside Catalyst—in fact, Catalyst didn't even have a data center or IT department because it had a best-partner relationship with SXC.

"Every step of the way, we had helped them succeed," Mark recalls. "We knew them for 10 years, like we knew ourselves—not just from a technology standpoint, but also their leadership team."

Conversations about a possible merger had taken place over the years. When it finally came together, it created value for both parties—plus $225 million in synergies realized from the combination of the companies. "We were their best partner, and we took that to the 'nth' degree and ultimately acquired the business. We were that good of a partner," Mark says.

Before the deal that created Catamaran, SXC had converted from a supplier of technology to a PBM, the same business that Catalyst was in. Rather than both parties becoming defensive, they became proactive best partners; Catalyst gained a seat on the SXC product advisory team, bringing together the best and brightest from both organizations.

"We were managing the business relationship at the highest level, getting to know our customer's businesses, their P&L, and operating structure," Mark says. "That was a best-partner role."

The culmination of that best partnership is catapulting growth, from $14.8 billion in 2013 (up 49 percent from 2012) to a projected $20 billion in 2014, thanks in part to a significant new best-partner customer.

In June 2013, Cigna Corporation announced that it had selected Catamaran to be its exclusive pharmacy benefit partner in what is described as a "strategic 10-year agreement to service the more than 8 million Cigna members." In its 2013 annual report, Catamaran described how the two companies "will partner on sourcing, fulfillment, and clinical services," by combining "Cigna's significant clinical management and customer engagement capabilities with Catamaran's innovative technology solutions."[4] The Cigna contract has been estimated to be worth more than $5 billion annually for Catamaran over a 10-year contract period.

Not surprising, it's a best-partnership model from the start: Cigna has a seat at the product design table with Catamaran, and both parties are discussing how Catamaran's pharmacy-benefits offerings mesh with Cigna's other strategic initiatives. When the Catamaran-Cigna partnership is fully implemented, Catamaran will have approximately 400 people dedicated to Cigna in a center of expertise.

The ultimate proof of the best partnership that Catamaran offered to Cigna is the fact that it was not the biggest player in this space. At the time of the deal, it had about a 5 percent share of the PBM market. "The odds were stacked against us," Mark says. After a nine-month selling process, Cigna was convinced that Catamaran

---

[4] Catamaran Corporation 2013 Annual Report.

was the best partner; as a result, Catamaran was able to significantly increase its market share.

"From a best partner standpoint, the Cigna win was proof positive," Mark says.

BEST PARTNERS

Best partnerships do not automatically happen, nor are they taken for granted. These relationships develop over time, with the realization and commitment by both parties that there is more value to be realized by working closely together. Best partnerships between a company and its customers (or, as we saw in Chapter 5, a company and its suppliers) may start by being transactional. One party is buying what another is selling. But they evolve beyond the transactional to the truly strategic and economic. Doing business together makes sense in terms of the value chain; efficiencies are realized and costs are reduced.

Ultimately, though, such partnerships can only be considered to be *best* when the benefits extend beyond the parties involved so the real beneficiary is the end user; then, the best just gets even better.

SECTION FOUR

BEST INVESTMENT

We cannot lose sight of the fact that every institution needs to earn a return for its stakeholders, not only financially, but with every resource it has—especially talent.

Every enterprise is focused on generating an attractive return for its owners. While this is certainly true of large, publicly traded organizations that are accountable to shareholders, it also applies to private companies with owners, as well as foundations and non-profits with supporters and benefactors. In every instance, organizations have to be accountable for how they generate a return, whether in terms of making money from the sale of products and services, or by wisely investing funds to fulfill a charitable mission. Furthermore and, I would argue, most important of all, every organization is accountable for how it attracts, develops, and deploys its most valuable resources—its talent—in order to become a *best investment.*

Best investment is the fourth of the bests in our continuum. Each phase of the process flows continually; we are always becoming our best selves, just as we continue to develop a best team and commit to best partnerships. It is only with these three bests in place on an ongoing basis that we can consider the fourth area: best investment.

131

In business, commerce, and charity, when people make a financial investment in an institution, they expect a return. Across a complex investment landscape in which one must consider interest rates, inflation, and the risks inherent in a challenging global economy, investors are looking for ways to increase their wealth so that they can buy a house, put their children through college, or prepare for retirement. Investors commit their money to an investment if they expect to earn a return as the enterprise executes its strategy.

The same holds true for not-for-profit institutions, such as an endowment fund. When I served on the board of one nonprofit organization, a senior staff member commented to the CEO, "Let's make no mistake; without money there is no mission." In the donor community, there is close scrutiny on every dollar that is invested by the nonprofit, as well as how the money is spent. Does 90 percent of the budget go to the cause that donors are supporting, or is only 20 or 30 percent going to that purpose? (As an aside, we can also think of how we spend our personal capital—whether we are squandering our resources, or saving and prudently investing for our future.)

How does an organization become *the best* in terms of investment, and how is that measured? Obviously investors have expectations for what happens to their money, and there is plenty of competition for investment capital. So how can an enterprise win in the investment war and capture its share of those dollars?

Making the challenge even more complex, there are competing priorities within every organization. A foundation often has to spend money (fundraiser galas, for example) in order to make money, while also making sure that it commits the lion's share of its budget to the specific cause it supports. A publicly traded company has to invest in new processes, technology, research and development (some of which will not be successful), marketing, recruitment, and so forth in order to advance the business. So how can an organization do all that—plus satisfy customers *and* earn a return that will satisfy investors? When we discuss these issues in my classes at Kellogg, often students assume that this is going to be extremely difficult because there is no way, given the competing interests, of keeping everybody happy. As many of them see it, at least initially, in order to *win* the investment war, some other group of constituents or stakeholders will have to *lose.*

Putting the principles of values-based leadership to work—especially by being *self-reflective* and gaining insight from *balance and perspective*—we grasp a holistic understanding of how all these pieces work together to deliver an optimal result.

In this section, we will discuss best investment from multiple viewpoints. First, Kelly Grier, Vice Chair, Talent, for EY Americas, will explain the importance of best investment from a talent perspective. If managers genuinely believe that talent is the best investment an organization can make, that attitude must drive decisions at the highest level, where visibility is the greatest across an organization. This is especially true in a professional services firm in which people must come first.

Next we will look at the generation of shareholder return and other hard and fast measures of best investment, from the perspective of two unique, but equally compelling viewpoints: Rick Waddell, chairman and CEO of Northern Trust Corporation, which has a market capitalization of $16 billion, and Tim Sullivan, a managing director of Madison Dearborn Partners, one of the leading private equity firms, with more than $18 billion in investments under management. They may approach best investment differently; Rick, as a CEO, is ultimately accountable to public shareholders, while Tim, as a private equity investment manager, seeks to generate a solid return from a portfolio of holdings for limited partners. Nonetheless, they both embrace values-based leadership, emphasizing integrity and sustainability over the long-term.

As we will see, when people in an organization become their best selves—that they understand their strengths and weaknesses so they can create best teams—and do business in a way that truly fosters best partnerships, the enterprise is on its way to becoming a best investment.

CHAPTER 7

MAKING A BEST INVESTMENT IN TALENT

I t all comes down to the people. Without them, no mission statement or corporate vision, no strategy, growth targets or performance goals, can ever be realized. Without human capital (or *talent*, which is the preferred term today) no other form of capital (e.g., money, equipment, intellectual property, etc.) can possibly produce a return. Therefore, we start our discussion of best investment with what matters most: the people.

As stated in the introduction to this section, every organization—large or small, public or private, for profit or not-for-profit, strives to generate a favorable return on investment. That return is not limited to the financial. In order to truly be a best investment, an organization must be a good steward of all its resources— especially the people who commit their time, talent, energy, and ideas to the enterprise.

It's not enough for management to say, "People are our best asset" or words to that effect. These words can quickly lose their power and begin to seem like lip service in an environment where companies are doing more with less, and downsizing is seen as necessary to increase profitability, and loyalty to an organization and to employees is considered a thing of the past. Despite all the proclaimed good intentions and mission statements about valuing people, the real priorities are communicated through an organization's actions.

Let's say that it's time for your regular performance review (monthly, quarterly, etc.). When you sit down with your manager, all she talks about is whether you and your team hit the financial goals. For example, if you are in sales, the boss spends 90 percent of the discussion on whether you met your quota. The people issues—how you are developing your team, how many people on your team have been promoted, and so forth—get only a brief mention, if any. Given the content of this discussion, it's quite clear what the real priorities of the organization are, as modeled by the boss's behavior. People, clearly, do not come first. Rather, it's all about the numbers. I'm reminded of the quote by industrialist Andrew Carnegie: "As I grow older, I pay less attention to what men say. I just watch what they do."

Where managers spend their time and put their emphasis sends a very clear message to other managers, team leaders, and individual contributors throughout the organization. The numbers and quotas are important, but if that's all the bosses talk about, to the exclusion of everything else, then everyone knows that those hard results are the only priority. As a consequence, in order to follow the boss's lead, others will dismiss the people issues as being the soft stuff. They will think and act based on the erroneous premise that focusing on people may be nice, but it won't move the needle in terms of performance and satisfying constituents as a best investment.

Nothing could be further from the truth. Obviously, the organization must generate top-line and bottom-line growth. But that can only be achieved as a consequence of having a best team (and best partnerships) in place. The prerequisites for becoming a best investment—of hitting the financial targets in a meaningful and sustainable way to the satisfaction of shareholders and other stakeholders—are attracting, retaining, and developing talent. In fact, how well a company develops its talent is a key component of becoming a best investment.

GETTING THE PRIORITIES RIGHT

If senior leadership genuinely believes that talent is the best investment an organization can make, that attitude must drive decisions at the highest levels, where visibility is the greatest across an organization. When I was a division president and later CFO and CEO, I knew that if I wanted my team to believe my words, my actions had to be consistent with what I said. On matters of values, culture, and talent, any discrepancy or inconsistency would throw into question my priorities and those of the organization.

A professional services firm, by definition, must be all about its people. After all, there are no manufacturing plants, no products coming off an assembly line. What a professional services firm is selling, ultimately, is the development and expertise of its people, aligned with the culture of the firm and equipped with intellectual property to address clients' needs. When it comes to being a best investment of talent, the professional services firm is a good example.

A leader in this space is the global organization Ernst & Young (EY), which has 190,000 people working in more than 160 countries. One of the shining stars in the company—someone I know and respect, who truly embraces the importance of talent development—is Kelly Grier, Vice Chair, Talent, for EY Americas.[1] In her position, she oversees the recruitment, engagement, and development of 54,000 people in the region. Her responsibilities include creating world-class learning, development, and coaching programs; fostering an inclusive and flexible culture; supporting career mobility; and maintaining the organization's focus on being

[1] Kelly Grier, telephone interview, July 25, 2014. All quotes and information come from Kelly Grier unless footnotes indicate otherwise.

an employer of choice in each of its markets. Kelly is also a member of the EY Americas Operating Executive and the EY Global Talent Executive Committees.

"In our business, we're all about the people who ultimately deliver the very best service we're capable of delivering to the marketplace," Kelly said. "Our people are how we differentiate our services from the competition and create greater demand for what we do."

Like any company, EY has quantitative targets and measures: market leadership, strength of the brand, revenue growth, profitability, and so forth, which must grow at least in pace with the market. But these goals and objectives cannot eclipse the people part of the performance equation. The challenge for any company in any industry is that the quantitative targets and measures tend to be more tangible than qualitative factors such as the impact of talent development. As a result, revenue, cost management, and profit targets can be more visible and, therefore, receive disproportionately more attention than talent management objectives. Successful organizations know that this cannot undermine efforts to support talent, the engagement and development of the team, and individual job satisfaction.

"We knew intuitively that really happy people who were enjoying the best experiences—who bought into the values and vision, who felt a strong connection with the team, and who had a strong commitment to the organization—would ultimately be manifested in world-class service delivery to our clients. And that would differentiate us from the competition. From there, we would grow our top line," Kelly says.

Balance is necessary. A company cannot focus only on talent development and ignore such things as top-line growth or managing costs. However, as Kelly describes it, the talent agenda has a "disproportionately large impact" on the financial results. "I have always found that if you can find one extra minute to invest, then invest it in your people to generate the biggest return," she adds.

Even when the payoff is not immediately visible, best-investment firms take it on faith that talent development will further the organization in accordance with its mission and vision. EY has quantified the economic benefits of having exceptional and highly engaged teams, linking talent to such hard numbers as a high-percentage growth rate and exceptionally strong margins. "You've got to have faith that when you differentially invest in the talent agenda, it's going to pay huge dividends," Kelly says. "Soon, that faith is replaced with empirical evidence. The results will follow. Then you will see that differential investment in talent will help you achieve your financial objectives as well."

Speaking to team members in venues such as town-hall meetings, Kelly addresses financial goals and results, but she makes the point that the financial data is "not what we do—it's the result of what we do." This is a very strong statement coming from a leader of a professional services organization who is also a CPA. Indeed, the fabric of the organization is very analytical and quantitative. But EY, which describes its purpose as "building a better working world," puts a genuine emphasis on having high-performing teams capable of delivering exceptional client service. In support of its purpose, EY has interrelated talent and performance goals, such as achieving "leading growth and competitive earnings sufficient to attract and retain world-class talent." That is exactly what it means to be a best investment.

SETTING THE "PEOPLE AGENDA"

With more than 23 years at EY, Kelly has held a number of leadership roles, including Chicago Managing Partner and Senior Advisory Partner for Ernst & Young LLP in the United States. She spent more than four years in EY's Zurich, Switzerland, office as coordinating partner, working with a Fortune 50 company and overseeing engagements in the Europe, Middle East, and Africa regions. She has also served on the firm's Americas Advisory

Council and the EY Global Advisory Council, which handle key matters in the Americas and globally.

EY emphasizes the importance of talent development and engagement by explicitly identifying *people-agenda* goals for team leaders, such as participation in recruitment, team development, and providing learning opportunities for team members. At the end of the year, people are asked to self-assess how they delivered on these objectives. As Kelly explains, goal-setting and account-ability are part of the infrastructure required to fulfill a talent agenda. "You can't just have someone preaching from the pulpit on this," she adds. "We do this through our goal-setting process, and with ongoing performance evaluation dialogue over the course of the year, and then through self-assessments and performance evaluations at the end of the year."

TALENT AND CULTURE

It's ironic that a company's most important asset—its talent—does not appear on the balance sheet, but that in no way devalues the contributions of the people who drive your business. An organiza-tion that is committed to being a best investment understands the importance of who is recruited, how those people are developed, what opportunities they are given to grow, and how they are rewarded for performance—in short, all aspects of culture.

Culture is how the organization defines itself internally, with expectations for how people interact and communicate with each other. Culture also has a strong external influence in how team members represent the organization to its partners (suppliers and customers), stakeholders, and the community at large. Without a values-based culture it is difficult for an organization to become a best investment, because it will fail to attract and retain the caliber of talent necessary to distinguish it from the competition.

As stated in our discussion of best teams, culture is the key to the health of any organization, from start-ups that are defining their vision and values, to large-scale corporate turnarounds that must realign a mature organization to its mission. From a best-investment perspective, having a strong, authentic, and clearly defined culture will help an organization attract and retain exceptional talent. Without true alignment, mission statements remain only words on paper, and not ideas to put into action.

It's not enough, however, to put culture in place and then assume it will thrive on its own—like a newly planted tree, it needs help taking root and getting water before it can grow. A culture left unattended can all too easily begin to crack and crumble. All it takes is a pattern of behavior inconsistent with the proposed value system. This will quickly become visible to others and undermine morale and culture.

WHERE IT FALLS APART

Without a firm and consistent commitment to culture, a company's values and priorities can be called into question or, in a worst-case scenario, dismissed as irrelevant or even false. As I describe in my first book, and I have seen in countless examples over the years, the first crack in the culture usually appears at the top. It may start with something seemingly harmless, such as looking the other way when someone who is a strong performer does something that is inconsistent with the organization's values. Even when the behavior is not unethical, the problem is the precedent it sets.

A friend of mine shared a story from early in her career at a publishing company in New York City in the late 1980s. The company had just instituted no-smoking rules, which were becoming the norm in those days. People could no longer smoke indoors, even in private offices with the door shut. Smoking was only allowed in certain designated areas outside. One editor, however, defied the rules by chain smoking in his office. As he blatantly told anyone who dared to remind him of the rule, "I'm a top performer here. I've been smoking in my office for years, and I'm not about to stop now."

He was, indeed, a top performer and a valued employee. So, the company looked the other way as the secondhand smoke drifted down the hallway—even when some employees, many of them in support functions, complained of health problems such as allergies and asthma. Other smokers obeyed the rules, but this top editor did not. The message that was sent across the organization was that if you were a strong performer, the no-smoking rule didn't apply to you. And if you were a support person, then you didn't matter at all.

I label this problem, "Bill, who doesn't get it" (and there are male and female "Bills" in organizations). Often, Bill is an amazing performer, generating incredible results—far exceeding the targets. Clearly, Bill is a real asset when it comes to making the numbers. The problem, though, is a lack of cultural fit; Bill just doesn't get it. Whether it's in the way he treats people, how he communicates with others, how he ignores certain directives around talent development, or even when he gets very near the line on ethical behavior (fuzzy expense reporting, for example), Bill is out of sync with the culture.

So what do you do with Bill? Can you make an exception? Do you let him shrug it off with that charming smile of his? Or do you fear what will happen if Bill leaves the company and goes to work for the competition? Having him on the other side, going after your accounts and prospects will be a formidable challenge. Is it just better to look the other way and rationalize that, in the grand scheme of things, Bill's performance is more important than the breaches in culture? (This can seem like a harder question to address when Bill's infraction is not outright illegal.)

Here's what I know to be true based on my career at Baxter International and through my talks with executives. Bill may be a strong performer, but his behavior undermines the culture in a serious and corrosive way. First of all, there are no secrets in the organization (just like how closing the chain-smoker's office door didn't stop the smoke from spreading). People will know. Then the real, unwritten culture of the organization becomes one of exceptions: If you can generate results and win awards, then you, too, can be the exception to the rules. As for all those words and statements about what the organization stands for and what its leaders believe (fairness, respect, cooperation, etc.), they are nothing more than happy talk.

Every leader encounters a Bill from time to time. Some leaders may find it hard to let someone like Bill go because of the loss of performance. The fact is, the damage Bill causes to the team in terms of morale, engagement, and belief in what the organization stands for far outweighs any short-term benefit of Bill's perform-ance (and it will be a short-term benefit. Someone who is out of sync with the culture will not be a strong performer for the long term). Therefore, as Kelly sees it, a leader who struggles with what is perceived to be a trade-off between culture and Bill's performance "is not quantifying all the economic consequences of Bill's behav-ior. The economic cost is invariably missing from the equation."

If Bill's behavior is unethical or illegal, he needs to be removed immediately. If Bill's behavior is out of sync with the culture (for example, the way he interacts or communicates with others) then the leader may decide that he needs to be educated, given clear expectations for his behavior, so there is no confusion, and a stern warning that any further breaches of culture will not be tolerated. Bill should also understand that, no matter how strong his per-formance—even if he's 200 percent of plan—if the objectionable behavior continues, he will be dismissed.

Coaching may help support Bill's cultural rehabilitation. He may be aligned with a partner or leader within the organization who demonstrates the desirable behaviors and values. These steps may be enough to turn Bill into someone who exemplifies the culture. In the process, he will also become a very visible example of just how seriously the organization takes cultural alignment, and how swiftly and decisively it will deal with breaches.

Over the years, I've seen some people turn their behavior around quickly. Perhaps the problem was a lack of understanding, or maybe a former boss told them something that was different from the organization's rules and norms. Once these people understood the expectations and the consequences, they immediately changed their behaviors to align with the culture. But in other instances, people were fired because they did not change, and the culture had to be protected.

Whatever the outcome, Bill should not be surprised. He should be given a clear explanation of the expectations and of the consequences. If Bill does not respect the values and culture of the organization, he has to go. Otherwise, the culture weakens and resentment builds, and the damage caused by tolerating Bill's behavior spreads through the organization like a cancer.

DEVELOPING TALENT

When an organization has a strong culture and places a premium on alignment across the organization, it establishes an optimal environment in which to develop talent. One way is by providing enriching experiences that enable individuals to learn, acquire new skills, and gain expertise. At EY, after a thorough vetting process that stresses cultural fit and values, people who join the firm are developed through an apprenticeship model, in which a less experienced person learns by working closely with those who have more skills and expertise. "We hire bright people, bring them on board, and then they learn so much on the job from the people they work for and with. They are constantly infused with experiences, learning, and coaching, which come from being part of a team," Kelly explains. "Experiential learning is a significant part of overall development."

EY also has a team structure that brings together people with varying degrees of experience, such as new hires, those who have been with the firm for 2 or 3 years, 4 to 5 years, 6 to 8 years, and partners who have 10, 20, or even 30 years of experience. "That's the kind of environment our people are working in," Kelly says. "It's really purposeful."

In addition, the firm makes sure that teams include people with varied competencies. For example, the audit practice brings together people with such diverse expertise as auditing, taxation, transaction valuation, and information technology (IT). "We have very integrated teams of people who can learn from one another. That's how people develop and how teams grow stronger," Kelly says.

Another aspect of its best investment in talent focuses on mobility in the broadest sense of that word, with international assignments. At EY, cultural diversity and having a global mindset are important values, which help to develop inclusive leadership. When leadership is inclusive, there is greater awareness of how decisions are made and their impact on people across the organization. Decisions may involve a change in strategy, an addition to or change in a service line, or even an acquisition. Companies that adopt a best-investment attitude around talent emphasize greater inclusiveness around setting goals and priorities, which will also foster greater buy-in.

Another benefit of a global mindset is greater appreciation for local culture within the context of organizational culture. As Kelly explains, "We have one brand, one common culture, and one common value statement around the world. We have a foundation that guides our every action. We all know what we stand for—our strategies, who we are, and what our values represent. How we ultimately effectuate the strategy or celebrate our culture, however, will be unique to some extent in each of our geographies around the world, so that it's authentic to who people are, as well as who they are as part of the EY family. That balance is hugely important to me."

Rather than trying to force one hard-wired model across every geography, with no accommodation for local cultural practice, being flexible and adaptable allows for some variation from location to location, which actually increases cultural adherence. "Otherwise, we would have more of a misaligned than an aligned organization," Kelly says.

Being flexible and adaptable does not mean compromising on foundational values or common culture. Rather, it establishes a foundation that is strong enough to allow variations on the theme, as a purpose-driven organization is constructed country to country and region to region. The result is a best-investment organization in which there is a bigger purpose that transcends individual cultural differences, creating a grand design of unity and alignment.

INTELLECTUAL AGILITY

Best investment in talent also occurs as silos break down, to expand understanding and experience across the organization. Kelly described this capability as "intellectual agility." As people move across functions or service lines, they gain skills, experiences, and competencies that enable them to move into positions of increasing responsibility. The optimal path of career development is a repeating pattern of horizontal and then vertical moves (across and up), like steps in a staircase. "These experiences challenge people's minds, broaden their capabilities, and grow their emotional intelligence," Kelly says.

Firms that take an intellectual-agility approach to talent development tend to be best investments because they discourage the silos that are created when the majority of people stick within specific roles or areas of competence. While such specialization does create in-depth expertise, it also limits the ability of people to represent the entire firm to a client. People in silos only speak the *dialect* of their one area; to be competitive in any industry or business today, people must be *multilingual*: able to express the full spectrum of an organization's services and products in ways that different audiences can understand.

Moreover, firms in any business are constantly changing, upgrading, redefining, and adding products and services in response to the changing needs of clients and other customers. In a professional-services firm, keeping pace with these changes requires teams of individuals who have intellectual agility and deep networks across service lines and geographies. "The relationships people have within

EY are almost or perhaps as important as the relationships they have with clients and the community, because that's how we hone that deep understanding," Kelly says.

The importance of an internal network brings to mind something that was told to me many years ago by William B. Graham, who joined Baxter in 1945 as a vice president and in 1953 became CEO. When I became CFO in 1993, Mr. Graham, who had served as CEO until 1980, asked me an intriguing question: "Suppose you were one of those people who thought they needed to know everything about a job before they were actually in the job. How long would it take to know everything to become a CEO?"

I told him, honestly, that I couldn't imagine.

"You'd be 185 years old," he laughed.

What Mr. Graham said to me next has stayed with me ever since: "If the company were to put someone in their forties in the CEO role, that person would only need to answer two important questions: The first is, what do I really know? The second is, who in the organization knows what I don't know?"

His sage advice emphasized the importance of developing connections across the firm, and using them to further one's intellectual agility. For example, someone facing a particular challenge or client need in the Midwest can reach out to colleagues on the West Coast or in Latin America, Europe, or Asia, to ask for advice and insights on how they tackled a problem or capitalized on an opportunity in their markets. Not only are such connections important on the individual level, but cultivating these relationships also helps organizations to become best investments of talent and other resources.

THE TEAM MINDSET: A BEST-INVESTMENT PERSPECTIVE

In my career, I have never referred to people as *employees*. I always speak about *teams* and *team members*. I wasn't trying to be cute, or to make people feel good by having them think, "Hey, I'm on the CEO's team." I meant it as much for myself as for them. It was one of the ways in which I acted as my best self. When I referred to the 52,000 people at Baxter as *team members,* I constantly reminded myself that we were all in it together as a best team, as a best partner with our customers and suppliers, and as a best investment, both financially (we discuss this in Chapter 8) and in how we developed talent. As I saw at Baxter and as I learn today from executives of large and small companies in many industries, when it comes to creating shareholder value, talent matters most.

For some people, though, it will seem counterintuitive that the more time, effort, and resources spent on talent development, the better the chance of becoming a best investment. The confusion is understandable, given all the pressure on people these days. In my classes at Northwestern University's Kellogg School of Management and in talks with executives, I often hear complaints such as: *I don't have enough time. I have to deliver on my projects. I can't be distracted by these people issues.* These comments are often made by very bright people who can read a financial statement backward and forward, and quote accounting standards from memory. The vast majority, if not all, of these managers and leaders want to do the right thing for their teams and their organizations. The problem is they feel so overwhelmed by all that needs to be accomplished that focusing on talent management becomes *one more thing* on an agenda that's already overly ambitious.

Then there is the pressure of the numbers, themselves. Even when senior leaders know that talent issues are important, with quarterly financial targets to make in order to satisfy shareholders and Wall Street, there is a strong temptation to let the short term eclipse the long term. Laying off several hundred or thousands of people may appear to be the only way to hit the numbers or provide proof that a reorganization is underway. Although companies do need the *right size* in response to the marketplace and economic conditions, organizations don't usually grow by cutting costs. And, what happens to the long-term performance when the remaining team members feel overwhelmed to the point that productivity decreases? How will a company attract the best talent when morale suffers and engagement declines? At the risk of repeating what should be obvious at this point, talent management matters the most.

When I was in senior leadership positions at Baxter, I was sometimes asked how much of my time I devoted to talent management. Taking into account the development of my team, communicating with people, and understanding who knew what across my network, it probably represented 95 percent of my time. People were sometimes shocked by my answer, and wanted to know how I managed to get everything done, if only 5 percent remained to do my work. They failed to grasp that the people part *was* my work! If I had the right people in place who knew what needed to be done, and who were highly motivated and engaged, then we would be on our way to success. By ensuring that my team was developing broader capabilities and getting the experiences they needed to take on new challenges and expanded responsibilities, I was furthering the growth of each individual and of the organization as a whole.

It can be difficult for some people to forge a connection between what they perceive as philosophical concepts and the need to make decisions and judgment calls. They tend to see binary choices between, say, talent development and performance targets. They do not see the synergies among developing talent, satisfying customers, and generating a return for shareholders. To them, if one switch is on then the others must be off.

Obviously, if an organization wants to be sustainable, it must increase sales, leverage costs, improve margins, and generate cash flow. These goals and objectives, however, are not mutually exclusive of talent development. Leaders must understand how everything in an organization ties together. Here, self-reflection can bring the leader back to what really matters for the long-term health of the organization: creating an optimal environment for the team, in order to generate more value for all stakeholders as a best investment.

In every organization—small or large, public or private, for-profit or not-for-profit, there is a direct link between talent and financial performance. Having great results is dependent upon having exceptional talent. This is the ultimate win–win all constituents and stakeholders enjoy when their organization becomes a best investment.

CHAPTER 8

THE PROOF POINT: SHAREHOLDER VALUE

I n the past seven chapters, we have explored and discussed becoming our best selves, forming best teams, forging best partnerships, and the importance of talent management as part of best investment. Along the way, a variety of leaders have shared compelling testimonies about the difference made by values-based leadership, as it emerges through self-reflection, balance and perspective, true self-confidence, and genuine humility. Now comes the moment of truth—or, shall we say, *proof*, as we turn our attention to being recognized by investors as a best investment.

If we want to assure ourselves that values-based leadership really does make a difference—elevating performance at every level, from the newest team member to the senior leadership team— we need to examine one measure: shareholder value. Shareholder value is one of those terms that everyone seems to kick around. Many executives like to say, "We are creating shareholder value," but what exactly does that mean? Some use the term shareholder value rather broadly, encompassing a variety of targets and milestones; others might use it to describe being the market leader in a particular industry or niche, or hitting a particular financial goal (e.g., becoming a $1 billion company generating a certain amount of net earnings). While all those goals can be attractive as they relate to the growth of the company, in and of themselves they do not reflect shareholder value. A company can boast that it has grown from $100 million to $200 million in revenue, or that it increased its earnings per share from $1.50 to $1.80, but that does not necessarily mean it is creating shareholder value.

By strict definition, shareholder value is generated when an investment made today is worth more in the future. I do not purchase a particular stock because I like the name or because I think it makes cool products. If, as an investor, I buy a stock for $30 a share today, the only economic reason is because I believe it will appreciate in value: from $30 to $35, $38, $40 and so on.

Shareholder value is composed of two parts: how much the stock has increased in price (otherwise known as stock apprecia- tion), and the amount of dividends paid to shareholders over a period of time. To express it as a formula, stock appreciation plus accumulated dividends equals *total shareholder return.*

It doesn't matter if the CEO says something fascinating at the annual meeting, or the chief marketing officer unveils a slick campaign for a new product, or the company publishes a beautiful annual report with charming pictures of children dancing in the sunlight—*show me the money!* That's why when I want to analyze how well a company is performing financially, I always turn to a chart in the annual report to answer a few key questions:

1. How much is my investment worth today versus when I purchased the stock? What is my total shareholder return over a specific period (one year, three years, etc.)?
2. How does my total shareholder return compare to bench- marks, both in the overall market and a peer group of similar investments? If a stock I purchased increased from $30 a share to $36, generating a 20 percent return, am I satisfied? What if during that period the total market increased 25 percent or a peer group produced a 50 percent return?

These same benchmarks—total return versus the market as a whole and total return versus a peer group—are also the measures by which professional investment managers gauge their own results. In financial terms, managers seek to generate *alpha*, meaning the amount of return that is over and above what is created by or attributable to the overall market. The more alpha that is generated on a risk-adjusted basis, the better job an investment manager is doing in selecting investments and managing a portfolio. While it is important to understand the company's sales and marketing programs, its investments in research & development, its planned investments in capital equipment, and its global strategy, these factors alone do not necessarily mean that shareholder value is being created. Rather, the sum of these efforts, if successfully executed, will be reflected in total shareholder return.

I hold values-based leadership to the same rigorous measure. If we really believe that the five bests (best self, best team, best partner, best investment, and best citizen) will improve financial performance, then the proof is in the total shareholder return they generate. Otherwise, the bests are only interesting concepts or *nice things to do*, but they cannot stand up to the measures that determine investment performance or create financial stability for an organization. It's like going to the doctor for your annual physical. You may be happy to report that you're walking more, eating green leafy vegetables, and drinking plenty of water, but if you're 25 pounds overweight, your cholesterol is 30 points higher, and your blood pressure is soaring, then what you're doing is not very effective!

The five bests, if done well, generate the kind of improvements that are critical to a successful organization. If not, then something is missing. Returning to our annual physical analogy, perhaps your healthy habits are being undermined by unhealthy ones, such as overindulging in the wrong foods. If we think we're doing our best in all areas, but the organization is not generating a shareholder return that is at least in line with its benchmark group, then we have to go back and reexamine our execution around each best.

In this chapter, we will discuss best investment from two unique, but equally compelling viewpoints: a CEO of a publicly traded financial institution and a managing director of a private equity firm. These two perspectives are provided to us by Rick Waddell, chairman and CEO of Northern Trust Corporation, which has a market capitalization of $16.5 billion, and Tim Sullivan, a managing director of Madison Dearborn Partners, one of the leading private equity firms, with more than $18 billion in investments under management. As a CEO, Rick is ultimately accountable to public shareholders, while Tim, as a private equity investment manager, seeks to generate a solid return from a portfolio of holdings for limited partners of endowment, pension, and sovereign wealth funds. They may approach best investment differently, but nonetheless, they both embrace values-based leadership, emphasizing integrity and sustainability over the long term.

NORTHERN TRUST: BUILDING SHAREHOLDER VALUE BY DOING THE RIGHT THING[1]

If producing shareholder return means generating a higher stock price over time, it would seem that management's priority would be to do everything in its power to increase revenues, decrease costs, and increase profitability and cash flow. There are times, however, when values-based leadership requires a counterintuitive approach in order to do the right thing and get the right results. In the short-term, this approach may mean taking a hit on revenue or profits, which could result in a reduction in stock price (this is usually short-term). Nonetheless, values-based leadership always puts the focus on doing the right thing, with the belief that actions will be recognized, and even rewarded, if not immediately, then over time.

---

[1] Rick Waddell, telephone interview, September 3, 2014. All quotes and data regarding Northern Trust Corporation come from this interview unless footnotes indicate otherwise.

Values-based leadership is always important and becomes imperative during the most challenging times, such as during the 2008–2009 financial crisis. As the new CEO of Northern Trust, Rick Waddell was just three months into his job when the first shock wave hit the financial markets in March of 2008: the near collapse of brokerage firm Bear Stearns (which was rescued in an 11th hour purchase). That was one of the warnings of just how vulnerable several large financial firms were to the fallout from risky investments in their portfolios. By the end of that year, several more firms were threatened with extinction, including Lehman Brothers, which went bankrupt. Through it all, Northern Trust remained solid, although not unscathed. "Just because we're Northern Trust and we're conservative, and we've been around for 125 years, doesn't mean that we were untouched by the financial crisis," Rick says.

Every financial firm, including Northern Trust, was impacted by the freezing of the credit markets, which brought buying and selling in fixed-income securities to a standstill. Even General Electric, a triple-A rated company, was unable to issue commercial paper (i.e., debt securities) because large institutional players were avoiding the credit market altogether. The challenge for Northern Trust was that, as a large custodial bank and asset manager, it held nearly $5 trillion in assets on behalf of clients (assets under custody and assets under management). During the crisis, certain Northern Trust asset management products came under stress. "It was a very tough time, operationally," Rick adds.

Northern Trust drew upon the expertise within the organization to examine the impact of the frozen credit markets given the extreme market conditions. The bank decided to "make it right for our clients," which it was able to do because of its financial strength—a hallmark of the firm from its earliest days. "We brought together the right people to figure out the solution, and then we used the financial strength of the company to fix the problem," Rick recalls.

Northern Trust also purchased some illiquid auction-rate securities from clients in its wealth management group, so that these individuals did not suffer a cash crunch because of the lack of liquidity in the credit market. "We did this for our clients who, otherwise, could not get access to their funds," Rick explains.

The purchased securities were held on the bank's balance sheet, and eventually became good investments, but only after several years as the markets gradually returned to normal. In the midst of the financial crisis, though, these securities were highly risky for the bank, because they could not be sold in the open market. By taking that risk and providing cash to its clients, Northern Trust demonstrated its commitment to excellent service.

Although noble, these actions were nonetheless costly for Northern Trust. After conferring with his predecessor, William Osborn, who at the time served as chairman of the board, and with the agreement of the board of directors, Rick and his senior leadership team authorized an accounting charge amounting to $561 million to support certain cash investment funds and clients who had invested in now-illiquid auction-rate securities. As a result, Northern Trust reported its first quarterly loss in 21 years. Rather than seeing it as a negative, those who knew the firm recognized it as a values-based action that would pay off in the long term. One securities analyst, for example, called it the best $561 million in "marketing expenses" that the bank could ever make to showcase its commitment to clients.

In keeping with his values-based leadership, Rick did not take a bonus in 2008, nor did the rest of the executive leadership team, because of the quarterly loss and the impact on shareholders. At the same time, while virtually every other large bank cut its dividend to conserve capital, Northern Trust did not—a positive for its shareholder return.

Today, the low interest rate environment makes it tough for banks to generate revenue. (Banks make money on the spread between the interest paid on deposits and the interest collected on loans.) Fortunately, net interest income is a small piece of Northern Trust's business (about 25 percent), while the other 75 percent or so is fee-based, including payment for fiduciary and asset management services. Because of the negligible yield on money-market funds, Northern Trust has waived a portion of its management fees on about $70 billion in short-duration money-market mutual funds. "The yields on those funds are so low we've had to waive much of our fees, because if we charged the whole fee, the yield would go negative. That cost us over $100 million in revenue in 2013," Rick adds.

Once again, though, in order to provide the best service to clients, Northern Trust has committed to doing the right thing, even though revenue is impacted, while trying to offset that impact by cutting expenses, improving efficiencies, and charging higher fees on some services. The bank set a two-year goal to improve pretax profits by $250 million, a target it exceeded with $270 million in profit improvements by the end of 2013.

Taking the high road has proved costly at times for Northern Trust, which might seem to fly in the face of being a best investment. However, the sacrifices it has made to support its clients have not hurt its long-term total return. For example, while most large banks have a price-to-earnings (P/E) ratio between 10 and 15, Northern Trust's P/E is 18. (P/E is the stock price divided by earnings per share and is used as a measure of a stock's value.) The high valuation is evidence that Northern Trust is a best investment, which Rick attributes to the bank's financial strength and the consistency of its earnings.

BECOMING A BEST INVESTMENT

The example at Northern Trust underscores the importance of looking at things holistically, and seeing beyond the impulse to make a knee-jerk reaction to make a short-term fix. When a best-investment attitude does not pervade an organization, however, short-term actions may be disconnected from the long-term impact, especially of becoming a best investment. First of all, some team members—someone in R&D, manufacturing, marketing, or sales—might say, "It would be nice to see the stock go up from $30 to $35, but that's the stock market. Those guys in New York are dealing with investors. What impact do I have on the stock price?"

A key requirement of leaders at all levels is to make sure that every person on the team can relate to total shareholder return. As discussed in Chapter 7, an organization needs to have the best talent in place. As we consider best investment from the perspective of shareholders, those talented team members must recognize that what they do each day impacts the organization's ability to become a best investment.

Across the total company, shareholder return is driven largely by increased cash flow from operations over time. Cash flow starts with sales, the top line of the company. What happens to that cash, though, depends on the ability of the company to manage its costs. Let's use a simple example: If a company sells widgets for $1.00 each, but it costs $0.99 to make them, that's not going to generate much cash! The company has to support its operations in the most efficient manner, from operating its plants to paying salaries and investing in product development. In addition, the company needs to make sure that its sales are bringing in cash by collecting receivables on a timely basis. The company also must manage its inventory so that it can meet customer demands, without having so much excess product on hand that it needs more costly warehouse space or risks having excess inventory that becomes obsolete. In addition, the organization needs to manage its capital expenditures so that it's investing in plant and equipment in a way that is consistent with demand, and in a part of the world that makes sense for operating costs and global logistics.

As stated earlier, the values-based organization that pursues the five bests cannot tolerate silo mentalities. In the language of the math major I once was, the optimization or maximization of the organization to generate shareholder return is *not* the sum of maximizing and optimizing individual silos. The individual business units, departments, and teams must come together and blend for optimal efficiency, the way an orchestra achieves balance in sound that truly makes beautiful music.

Let's look at some specific examples. If you talk to people on the sales team, it doesn't take long to explain that a key component of shareholder value is generated by sales. A typical response from a team member might be, "I've got that, chief. I'm going to sell more!" Well, yes, sell more. But it's very important to consider the price at which you're selling the product. If prices are cut dramatically, the organization may sell more, but the margin, which has a direct impact on cash flow, will suffer. It's not just a case of selling more, but in what quantities and at what price to what best partners need to be considered to optimize the entire value chain.

If you talk to the folks in manufacturing, a plant manager would love to figure out a way to minimize costs. If he can reduce the unit cost from $0.99 to $0.90 then, all other things being equal, the margin will be higher and more cash flow will be generated. But all things are *not* equal. If reducing the cost can only be accomplished by, say, doubling the number of hours that the plant runs, what will happen to the extra inventory produced? Will the organization have to build more warehouses, or find other places to store the inventory? And don't forget inventory carrying costs. What started out as a way to lower manufacturing expenses could end up increasing the total cost in the value chain, and adversely impacting cash flow and stock price.

Now, let's broaden the conversation by bringing in human resources. These folks realize that lower operating expenses will lead to increased profits and higher cash flow, and could potentially lead to an increase in the stock price. The question then becomes, how do we reduce operating expenses? With a silo mentality, human resources might see the potential to reduce the number of team members. But what is the impact of the knowledge lost when experienced people leave? What happens to morale among those who are left? Will the company be properly staffed to handle current demand? If there aren't enough people in the right jobs to get the work done, will sales decrease, will manufacturing costs increase?

As these simple examples show, attempts to reduce operating expenses can end up *hurting* cash flow, and therefore lead to a lower stock price. When a company is committed to being a best investment, it takes the time to educate team members about how to improve shareholder value and all the factors that directly influence it. When people embrace the fact that what they do impacts the entire organization, the silos come down, and thinking expands to what is in the best interest of the entire organization.

TYING INCENTIVES TO BECOMING A BEST INVESTMENT

One way to increase team members' understanding of shareholder value is to tie incentives to best investment. It's one thing to say to a team member, "I want you to do things that will increase shareholder value." But if that person cannot directly relate to how that happens, or if someone is not rewarded for contributing to that goal, it's harder to motivate people. Incentives help make total shareholder return more than just a number that is watched by *those guys* in finance. At Baxter, one of the ways we closed that gap in understanding was to provide every team member, at every level in the company, with stock options. In effect, every team member became more closely aligned with other shareholders. When the company performed well and the stock price appreciated, the team members also benefited. And, it worked both ways. When the stock price declined, they felt the negative impact.

Another example of aligning employee and shareholder interests is Northern Trust. In 1988, Wes Christopherson, who was CEO at the time, put in place an employee stock ownership plan (ESOP), whereby 10 percent of the company was given to employees, with stock vesting over 10 years. At the time, the market capitalization of the bank was $650 million, meaning the 10 percent ESOP ownership had an initial value of $65 million. Today, given Northern Trust's market cap of $16 billion, the 10 percent ESOP stake is worth $1.6 billion. With team members so closely aligned with the company, and being cognizant of creating (and benefiting from) shareholder value, it's no surprise that long careers are common at Northern Trust, as evidenced by its Quarter Century Club. People who have been with the bank for 25 years are recognized at a reception and given a 25-year medallion and gift. Most years, 90 to 130 people at Northern Trust mark their 25th anniversary with the company. In 2014, there were 138 inductees to the Quarter Century Club; there were 97 in 2013. "Those impressive numbers got me thinking? What was going on 25 years ago? That's when the ESOP had just been put in place," Rick comments.

In a values-based organization, as team members come to a fuller understanding of how their roles and job functions contribute to best investment, the importance of communication cannot be overestimated. Internally and externally, stakeholders need to have a good understanding of what the organization is doing and how that relates to being a best investment.

In a publicly traded company, the CEO and the CFO hold conference calls every quarter to inform shareholders about the organization's performance over the past 90 days: what went well and what didn't go as well, and what are the plans to enhance shareholder value to become a best investment in the future? Many executives view these quarterly calls as an annoying but necessary part of doing business as a publicly traded company. In my time at Baxter, I had a different perspective. To my thinking, shareholders are the owners of the company. And if these people invested their money in our organization, in hopes of earning a return to fund their homes, retirements, and their children's education, we owed them the opportunity to understand how we were doing, both in the short term and the long term.

One reason to take issue with these quarterly calls is if they encourage very short-term thinking. Becoming a best investment requires a holistic perspective. That does not mean that leaders can ignore the short-term. As I like to joke, if a company has to choose between the short-term and the long-term, the answer is "yes"—in other words, they have to focus on both. But sacrificing the long-term for the sake of only *looking* good in the short-term does not usually result in becoming a best investment.

Part of the education of shareholders, therefore, is explaining to them how the company is managing short-term expectations and long-term growth. Sometimes the two will be aligned: short-term results will be positive as the company pursues its long-term objectives. Other times, short-term results may not be as strong because, for example, the company is making a significant investment in capital equipment or increasing R&D that will generate a return in the future. My strong belief was that if we could clearly explain what we were doing and why, shareholders would understand. If we built trust and credibility with investors, our stock price would likely increase, boosting total shareholder return, because of the merits of our long-term strategy, even when the short-term financial results fell short of expectations.

Sometimes people say to me, "That all sounds great, Harry, but in the real world investors and analysts might not be so forgiving of a short-term disappointment. They are very short-term oriented." My response to these comments is to ask the question: How do you explain stocks such as Amazon or Facebook, both of which went through periods of generating very little cash flow and earnings, and yet enjoyed market capitalizations in the billions of dollars? If the markets were so short-term in orientation, there would never be companies with negative cash flow that generate significant shareholder returns. It's not that the market doesn't care about cash flow. It's that if company leadership can convince investors that investments today will generate future cash flows on a net present-value basis (i.e., converting future cash flows into present dollars) the result can be an increasing stock price.

Looking at another example, let's say that a company's stock is trading at $50 a share when it announces that it's making an acquisition. In the short term, let's assume that the acquisition will be dilutive (earnings per share will decrease), but the deal makes great economic sense long term. If the company doesn't explain why purchasing the firm is a good economic investment, the only thing shareholders will see is a short-term reduction of cash flow and earnings. Without a compelling explanation, the stock could very well fall to, say, $45 or $40 a share.

If the company is committed to being a best investment, it will take the time and make the effort to communicate to all stakeholders why a certain deal makes sense and how it will add to future growth and cash flow. If the organization has proven in the past that it can successfully integrate an acquisition (as explained in Chapter 6), then the stock price may not be adversely affected and could increase, despite the short-term dilutive effect on earnings. However, if the company doesn't have a strong track record of successfully making acquisitions, then the company shouldn't be surprised if investors react negatively to an announcement of an acquisition that reduces short-term results.

PRIVATE EQUITY: THE INVESTOR POINT-OF-VIEW

Private equity firms are in the business of finding opportunities in which to invest on behalf of limited partnership investors that include endowment, pension, and sovereign wealth funds. At Madison Dearborn, we focus on value-oriented businesses (those that are currently undervalued compared to the value of their assets), as well as growth-oriented companies. Our investment strategy focuses primarily on the quality of the business, its prospects for the future, and its leadership.

As I've seen with many companies in the Madison Dearborn investment portfolio, values-based leadership enhances the attractiveness of a company, making it a prime candidate to generate an above-market return, also called *alpha.* "An alpha-performing company will attract the investment capital it needs to grow the business,"[2] comments Tim Sullivan, a managing director at Madison Dearborn, where he heads the MDP Health Care practice. "The only way to do that is by attracting the talent to create best teams, having a culture that values best partnerships, and then outperforming as a best investment."

By focusing on companies that exhibit values-based leadership and the five bests, Tim adds, there is a greater chance that these organizations will stand the test of time. "We look for companies that will thrive, even beyond our ownership." A best-investment portfolio company will not only produce a strong return for private equity investors, but will continue to do so beyond their ownership.

Tim describes his criteria for finding a best investment as the "5 Cs":

1. **Competency:** The leadership team's expertise and knowledge of their industry and the competition
2. **Courage:** The ability to make tough decisions, even to sacrifice in the short term if that proves best for the long term
3. **Compassion:** Caring about people who work for the firm, knowing them as individuals and developing their careers
4. **Culture:** The mission, vision, and values that will attract and retain the best talent
5. **Communication:** Ensuring that the culture, mission, values, and other priorities are not only understood at the senior leadership level, but throughout the organization

[2] Tim Sullivan, telephone interview, August 29, 2014. All Tim Sullivan quotes come from this interview unless footnotes indicate otherwise.

Beyond the numbers alone (e.g., the "valuation metric"), Tim looks for companies and leadership teams that are strong in all 5 Cs, which he calls "qualitative metrics." He then looks to enhance the 5 Cs with an ownership mentality of accountability and performance as a result of the investment structure that private equity puts in place as part of an acquisition. Ideally, a company will show some degree of strength in all five areas, and not just in one or two. For example, it's not enough for the leader of the company to have a high degree of competency, as evidenced by his industry knowledge and understanding of the competitive landscape, if he does not exhibit compassion for his team, such as deferring to others for their input. (In a meeting with 10 of the company's senior leaders and top managers, if the CEO does all the talking, that's not a sign of a compassionate/caring culture that elevates people and encourages their development.) In addition, if all the knowledge rests only with the CEO and a few other top leaders, communication does not appear to be valued in that company. Beyond these cultural implications, a leadership team that is dominated by the CEO raises concerns about succession issues. Are there people groomed and capable to step into senior positions?

Finally, the search for a best investment must meet Tim's criteria of "industry, company, management, and deal." Starting with industry, Tim holds the view that any market sector is only as strong as its weakest competitor. "We look at the competitive dynamics. How does the competition compete? Is it a growing industry or is it shrinking? Even if you are a best-in-class buggy-whip manufacturer with significant share of market, that doesn't mean much if the internal combustion engine has just been invented," he quips.

Moving from industry to company, the favored investment candidates tend to be those with a market leadership position, or that have other strong competitive advantages, such as innovative, *disruptive* technology that will bring about change in an industry or create a new niche.

With management, Tim looks for leaders who are well matched with the stage of the company. For example, the founder or entrepreneur may have been perfect to launch and grow the company, but is she the best leader now that the firm is at the next stage of maturity? "Marrying and matching the stage of the company with the right leadership is important in making an investment," Tim explains.

Finally, the deal has to make sense. A prospect may look great in terms of industry, company, and management. However, if the asking price is higher than the company is worth, it is not going to be a best investment. "You love the business—maybe it's the best thing you've ever seen. But if the pricing doesn't work, you shouldn't make the investment," Tim adds.

For Tim, doing the right thing on behalf of investors means remaining diligent to find best investments, given the long-term time horizon of a private equity deal. This discipline is best served with a values-based leadership mindset. With genuine humility, the investment manager is prepared to listen to others, such as trusted advisors, while having the true self-confidence not to succumb to a herd mentality. Self-reflection continuously orients the investment manager to do the right thing, for the benefit of all involved.

THE TEST OF THE BEST

If we start with the premise that values-based leadership is critical to elevating the performance of the team, then the proof will be evident, and in more ways than just subjective or *soft* metrics. While the five bests may be inspiring, or make people may feel good about themselves and their organizations, the ultimate proof is in the numbers.

A values-based organization that commits to the five bests has a good chance of achieving consistent growth in its sales, earnings, cash flow, and stock price. As a result, it will become a healthy enterprise with a positive track record, positioning itself as a best investment.

BEST CITIZEN

As an organization becomes a best citizen, everyone from senior leaders to the most junior level is focused on both success and significance.

Each of the five bests is a journey, and having addressed four of them (best self, best team, best partner, and best investment) we've come a long way. Consider what we've accomplished so far. By becoming our best selves, we embrace and embody the four principles of values-based leadership: self-reflection, balance and perspective, true self-confidence, and genuine humility. Through best teams, best partners, and best investments, we use values-based leadership to make a measurable difference in our organization. At this point, it's tempting to say, "Pencils down, we're done!" We still, however, have one more important *best* to address—that of best citizen.

Being a best citizen means taking on the challenge of making the world a better place. Rather than expecting others to do the work, best citizens—whether individuals or organizations—ask themselves what they can do to make a difference. Often, this is a shift in thinking that leads us to put our values into action in significant ways.

Many times when people gather socially or professionally, the conversation leads to how fortunate many of us are and the needs of those less fortunate. There may be a particular story in the news that relates to global poverty, world hunger, health-care issues, the digital divide, or environmental concerns. Sometimes these discussions become very emotional, or even heated, as people express their opinions that these important issues absolutely must be addressed by *someone*. People are often quick to assign that responsibility, whether to the government, philanthropists, or nongovernmental organizations (NGOs)—all of which come under the heading of *those guys*. People expect this infamous group of men and women who are somewhere out there to take ownership of the problems and address them. But as we know, *those guys* are not just *out there*. They're *right here*; in fact, *we* are *those guys*!

Values-based leadership and the five bests not only teach us how to avoid dwelling on what others can or should be doing, but also to ask ourselves the question: What can I (as an individual and/or as a leader at any level of an organization) do to make a difference in the world? If someone needs to do something then why can't that *something* begin with me? As values-driven individuals we see it as our responsibility to make the world a better place in big and small ways. In fact, if we live our values, we cannot stop at the realization that issues exist; we are obligated to do something about them. We are committed to play a positive role in changing even one thing, no matter how small or locally focused it may be.

As we will learn in the next two chapters, becoming a best citizen is both a corporate mission and a personal goal. On the corporate side, we will address the long legacy of philanthropy at Target Corporation, which since 1946 has contributed 5 percent of its profits annually to local, national, and global causes that matter most to its customers and team members.

For many organizations like Target, being a best citizen leads to social responsibility and making a difference in the communities and countries in which they operate. It can also lead to supporting important global initiatives (which, incidentally, often require best partners). While profitability and success are important, being a best citizen becomes a unifying element in the corporate culture. People see their jobs in the context of the bigger, broader purpose of making a positive change in the world.

On an individual level, being a best citizen can be a personal mission, as it is for Andrew Youn, who, after graduating with his MBA from Northwestern University's Kellogg School of Management in 2006, took on the huge challenge of addressing poverty and hunger among East African farmers. Today, One Acre Fund, which Andrew co-founded, serves more than 200,000 farm families in Kenya, Rwanda, Tanzania, and other African countries.

There is no shortage of problems in the world that need to be addressed. Trying to tackle too many too quickly becomes daunting. Rather than run the risk of becoming overwhelmed, we can use self-reflection to help us identify where we have the most passion and where we can make the most impact. It does not matter if our individual efforts are local, such as volunteering to support a cause or helping an organization that we feel passionate about, or if, as a values-based leader of an organization, we can take on significant issues affecting a community or country in which we do business.

Also in our discussion, we will explore how organizations can take social responsibility to the next level, going beyond the good things that they believe they *should* do, to achieving greater integration between social and business agendas—even to the point of seeing them as one agenda. Here, we encounter the concept of "shared value," as explained by Harvard University's Michael Porter and Mark Kramer. With shared value, what is good for the community is good for the business, and vice versa—even to the point of reinventing the business agenda.

But first your organization must become a best citizen and ask the compelling question that continuously drives the discussion, internally and externally: *What can we do to contribute to our community and the world that will also be positive for the organization?*

Every effort matters. Together, as values-based leaders, we can make an enormous difference—leaving a positive global footprint, changing the world around us and the lives of others. After all, we are *those guys;* what are we waiting for?

CHAPTER 9

VALUES IN ACTION

B ecoming a best citizen, may look like another one of those *nice things* that companies can do, from the local merchant who sponsors a little league team, to a multibillion-dollar global enterprise that establishes a foundation to support various causes. With this thinking, we might consider best citizenship as something a company can *afford* to do because it's done so well with the other four bests (best self, best team, best partner, and best investment). While this perception is, perhaps, understandable, it is nonetheless inaccurate. Rather than being the icing on a corporate cake, becoming a best citizen is a key ingredient in values-based leadership for the individual and the organization.

From a holistic perspective, we see that there is an inter-relationship among all five bests in a values-based organization: best teams and best partners enhance best investment; best citizenship enables the recruitment and retention of best teams and solidifies best partnerships; and becoming one's best self provides the foundation for every best effort. The desire to make the world a better place resonates deeply with individuals as they become their best selves. Among my students at Northwestern University's Kellogg

School of Management, I find many who are highly motivated by causes and the desire to make a difference, whether that shapes their careers or informs their personal choices. Organizations should encourage team members to put their values in action at work, rather than asking for those values to be set aside, or postponed to be addressed later. Being a best self isn't something you put on or take off like a raincoat, as you move from personal life to work life. (The concept of *work/life balance* has always confused and amused me, since it seems to imply that one is either working or living. Isn't work part of life?) Best citizenship, therefore, honors the integration of best self into every other "best," as the fullest expression of values-based leadership. Or, as William Graham, the long-time CEO of Baxter International used to say, "We are blessed to do well by doing good."

Among values-based organizations that are truly best citizens, one that stands out for the depth and longevity of its commitment is Target Corporation, the Minneapolis-based retailer. Target has a long history of giving back, with activities that fall under the umbrella of corporate responsibility, from sustainability to promoting employee wellness, and supporting education initiatives in K-12 schools.

"An organization can do well financially and generate the kind of shareholder return that it should, while still doing good in the community. These are not mutually exclusive concepts,"[1] says Laysha Ward, president of Community Relations for Target Corporation and a member of its leadership team. Reflecting the values of Target's founders, the company has donated five percent of its profits annually to charity since 1946. "It's part of the DNA of the company," Laysha adds. "It's why we are a purpose-driven company."

---

[1] Laysha Ward, telephone interview, September 5, 2014. Quotes and data regarding Target Corporation come from this interview unless footnotes indicate otherwise.

A SHIFT IN THINKING

Embracing best citizenship as being integral to becoming a values-based leader and a world-class organization may require a shift in thinking. It's easier, perhaps, to see how becoming one's best self, forming best teams, forging best partnerships, and becoming a best investment improve the organization at all levels. But best citizenship may not appear to have an obvious connection. For one thing, as we discussed in Chapters 7 and 8 on best investment, values-based leadership must contribute to an organization's ability to generate a return. On that basis alone we might question how best citizenship meets that same criterion. After all, there is definitely an expense, and typically a significant one, involved in philanthropic giving. Donations and grants cost money, reduce profits, and could, conceivably, lead to a lower stock price.

Some senior leaders, in the spirit of upholding their fiduciary responsibilities (which they must take seriously), may be troubled by what looks like a trade-off between profits and philanthropy. Furthermore, having reached what feels like a pinnacle with best investment—individual people feel good, teams feel good, partners feel good, and the stock price is increasing—there is an understandable temptation to declare victory. Having achieved best investment, we are standing on what looks like a summit. We have arrived!

Great economic minds, the likes of Milton Friedman, agree. They argue, as many of us learned in finance classes, that the role of a manager in a company is to generate shareholder value. A company's returns, therefore, ought to benefit shareholders and are not for management to spend on something as seemingly discretionary as philanthropy. Admittedly, when you look at things narrowly, a $1 million philanthropic donation reduces a company's earnings by $1 million. To that way of thinking, it would seem better to give that $1 million to shareholders and then let them decide how and where to spend their money, rather than having the company make donations on shareholders' behalf.

However, I do not think that the journey of values-based leadership ends with best investment. By engaging in self-reflection, we see that values-based leadership means more than just generating a return for shareholders. Therefore, the pertinent question to consider isn't whether to be a best investment *or* a best citizen; you need to become both. As we stand on the platform of having become a best investment, we realize that what looked like the summit is really another base camp. As we look around, ready to congratulate each other on how far we've come, we acknowledge that the journey continues. There are significant global societal issues all around us, in developing countries and in our own backyard, that demand our attention. As stated in the introduction to this section on best citizenship, we recognize that we can't expect *those guys* to tackle the major issues facing the world. *We are those guys,* and it's up to us to do something.

The answer for many organizations is to take up the cause of social responsibility. In fact, in the corporate world, the concept of being a best citizen is often seen as synonymous with social responsibility. In essence, social responsibility reflects the theory that organizations and individuals have a responsibility to contribute to the benefit of society. In fact, the for-profit and nonprofit worlds have much in common in achieving their mission and vision as best citizens. As Rob Thielen, in a column for *Forbes* observed:

> . . . *Business and charitable work can be complementary, as many of the most well-known foundations prove, often using business metrics to assess performance and effectiveness. This is because while the fundamental goals of business success and venture philanthropy may differ (making money and growing your business and profits vs. raising money and assisting a non-profit cause) the ways in which these goals can be achieved remain the same: having a clear purpose, good management, a strong team, hard work and dedication.*[2]

[2] Rob Thielen, "The Business of Charity—Four Drivers to Succeed," *Forbes Online,* September 2, 2014.

To many who embrace social responsibility (also known as *corporate social responsibility*), the more resources at an organization's (or individual's) disposal, the greater the expectation (and, often, pressure) that a portion of those resources be spent on doing good works and supporting worthy causes. This has given rise to various listings and rankings of the most socially responsible companies, based on such measures as philanthropy and sustainability. There is also a growing trend in socially responsible investing, in which investors put their money in companies that share their same philosophical values. With this in mind, socially responsible activities can protect or improve an organization's reputation—and even enhance its status as a best investment.

Corporate and organizational support for various social causes is admirable and necessary, especially as private funds make up for a shortfall in government support for social causes and initiatives, given tighter budgets on the federal, state, and local levels. But social responsibility, itself, is an evolving concept. The next phase may very well be to embrace a broader purpose in what we think of as social responsibility, to become what Harvard University's Michael Porter and Mark Kramer describe as "shared value."

Porter and Kramer define shared value "as policies and operating practices that enhance the competitiveness of a company while simultaneously advancing the economic and social conditions in the communities in which it operates." As the authors explain, whereas social responsibility puts "societal issues . . . at the periphery, not the core," shared value creates "economic value in a way that *also* creates value for society by addressing its needs and challenges . . . Shared value is not social responsibility, philanthropy, or even sustainability, but a new way to achieve economic success. It is not on the margin of what companies do but at the center."[3]

[3] Michael E. Porter and Mark R. Kramer, "Creating Shared Value," *Harvard Business Review*, January-February 2011.

So how can organizations and individuals get to a place of greater integration between social and business agendas—even to the point of seeing them as one agenda? I believe it starts with becoming a best citizen. The word best signifies that this is a journey—just as it is for self, team, partner, and investment. Organizations, large and small, are already citizens of the communities and countries in which they do business. Becoming a best citizen builds upon that physical presence and asks the questions: What can we do to contribute to the community and the world that will also be positive for the organization? Can both happen simultaneously?

By understanding shared value we realize the development of a community—addressing such issues as hunger, poverty, health, education, and the environment—is also good for business. When people are healthier, well educated, and have a safe place to live, they become part of a stronger population base of consumers and potential employees. Everyone benefits.

AUTHENTICITY CREATES ALIGNMENT

To the extent that individuals and organizations strive to be values-based, best citizenship must be authentic and pursued in the right spirit. While there is a marketing aspect to supporting a particular cause or initiative—and getting on the list of gold or platinum sponsors—best citizenship isn't the same as putting the company name on a sports arena or erecting a billboard. If philanthropic actions are not sincere, no matter how generous they might be, people will see right through them. Instead of inspiration, a company will generate cynicism.

The key is alignment. As a member of a community, an organization takes up causes that matter most *to that community*. Authenticity creates alignment. When an organization champions causes that matter most to people who work there (best team members) and those who do business with it (best partners, including suppliers and customers), that is truly best citizenship in action.

A recent column in *Forbes* cited the Ice Bucket Challenge, which went viral on the Internet, raising awareness and donations for ALS (amyotrophic lateral sclerosis, or Lou Gehrig's Disease). Soon, politicians, sports teams, and ordinary folks were recording videos of themselves dumping buckets of ice water over their heads—and then challenging others to do the same. Companies, too, joined in. It was a successful example of viral, peer-to-peer marketing, creating a powerful buzz in support of an important cause. This led *Forbes* columnist David Hessekiel to pose a question well worth asking: "What if companies could marry the individual engagement of these peer to peer fundraising efforts with their own corporate citizenship programs to move the needle on their own business objectives as well as a social cause?"[4]

Companies that are already active in the charitable space, such as by being sponsors of corporate challenges, Toys for Tots, or annual food drives, are no doubt familiar with the halo effect that can be created through participation in such activities. Engendering goodwill can increase an organization's visibility in the community and also increase customer loyalty and enhance a brand's image. Once again, an organization's authentic connection with the community and its priorities is what makes these activities part of best citizenship. "By more fully integrating a cause into every aspect of their business, a company is able to tell an intentional, ongoing story about their commitment to a cause and bring customers alongside them," Hessekiel adds.[5]

Commitment, I would suggest, is the operative word. As with almost everything in life, self-reflection will foster discernment: understanding what the organization is doing and why, and what it expects in return (i.e. to motivate best teams and best partners, or simply to look good).

[4] David Hessekiel, "How Your Company Can Lead the Consumer Cause-Marketing Charge," *Forbes Online*, September 11, 2014.
[5] Hessekiel, "How Your Company Can Lead the Consumer Cause-Marketing Charge."

LEAD WITH A PURPOSE

Today, with more than $70 billion in revenue, thousands of vendor partners, and hundreds of thousands of team members, Target makes a significant philanthropic commitment, amounting to $4 million a week. Its corporate giving, Target believes, benefits all stakeholders—from team members to suppliers to customers (or *guests*, as Target calls them). "If you lead with a clear, compelling, and actionable purpose, something that people can get behind and want to be part of, the results will follow," Laysha said.

Target's corporate responsibility touches many important issues. A message posted on the company's web site discusses various sustainability initiatives, including: providing "more responsibly sourced, wellness-focused food"; using the Higg Index (a sustainability measurement tool used primarily by apparel and footwear companies) to assess thousands of vendor partner facilities; achieving LEED (Leadership in Energy and Environmental Design) certification for each of the 124 stores Target opened recently in Canada; and sharing its experiences "to help the industry proactively address and prevent crime in the digital space."[6]

Over the years, I've gotten to know Target's senior management and their commitment to values-based leadership, and I can attest that the organization's goals and actions around sustainability and corporate responsibility are not just window dressing. Target has a deep commitment to elevating the way in which it does business. Moreover, by spending time with Target executives and making a presentation on values-based leadership to Target's leadership team, I've witnessed first-hand the company's commitment to developing its team members. It is clear that Target's focus is to enable each team member to become their best self, support one another, and treat one another as guests of their stores.

[6] Target Corporation. "A Message from Target," Target.com web site, 2014.

"Our team members are our greatest asset," says Laysha, who, many years ago, worked at a Target retail store in Chicago, where she first experienced the company being part of a local community. (She later earned a bachelor's degree in journalism from Indiana University and a master's degree in social services administration from the University of Chicago.) "Being locally relevant is really important if an organization is going to be purpose-driven and values-based," she adds.

Development of its team members, in fact, is one way in which Target sees itself giving back to the local community. "We try to unleash the power and potential of all our team members— nurturing them and building their skills to become leaders. We think this is one of the greatest gifts we can provide to our company and to the world," Laysha says. As people become their best selves and join together in best teams, they can do extraordinary things not only within the company, but also within their families and communities. "The ripple effect is tremendous," she adds.

Team-member empowerment also helps with focus and effectiveness in best citizenship. As stated in the introduction to this section, organizations cannot do everything. In fact, the trend in overall corporate giving and social responsibility has been to support fewer causes and initiatives, but to do so in a bigger way to increase the impact. As an organization chooses where to spend its time and talent—on a corporate level and also among its team members—it naturally gravitates to activities with which it has a natural affinity, locally or globally (for example, a grocery store that makes donations to a food pantry, or a pharmaceutical company that supports global health initiatives). When the decision of how and where to commit resources involves the entire organization, commitment becomes broader and deeper.

Target's philanthropic efforts start with listening to its guests and its team members, discerning what means most to them and to the communities in which they work and live. "Based on those insights, we make sure our strategic intent is aligned with their expectations and with our unique capabilities as a business," Laysha says. "We believe business can be part of developing solutions for pressing social issues, and we strive to create shared value through initiatives that provide solutions for guests and meaningful benefits to both business and communities."

The willingness to listen to guests and team members calls to mind the four principles of values-based leadership: self-reflection to establish priorities; balance and perspective to seek feedback from others; true self-confidence to make the decisions and commitments necessary; and genuine humility to keep an ear to the ground for feedback and to respect all people.

TARGETING EDUCATION

After listening to others, Target commits the lion's share of its philanthropy to supporting K–12 education, with a goal of spending a cumulative $1 billion in support of education as of fiscal year-end 2015. The company's Take Charge of Education program aims to donate an additional $425 million to schools by the end of 2015. Take Charge of Education funds are nondiscretionary, meaning schools can spend the money wherever it's needed. "These kinds of funds are difficult to come by for schools," Laysha says.

Believing that a focus on education is critical for the United States to remain innovative, stay globally competitive, and build leaders of the future, Target has set its sights on supporting students from pre-kindergarten through elementary and secondary grades, all the way to high-school graduation—and beyond. Attaining advanced educational goals is only possible with a strong foundation, which for students at risk means early childhood literacy intervention. Target cites statistics that children who can't read proficiently by the end of third grade are four times more likely to drop out of high school than children who can.

The objective of Target's education initiatives is to help students stay on the path to completing high school, with the goal of helping to raise the overall graduation rate in the United States from 81 percent to 90 percent, in line with America's Promise Alliance's GradNation program. The graduation rate among minority students is especially troubling, at 68 percent for African-American students and 73 percent for Hispanic students. "The achievement gap between white students and those of color persists," Laysha says.

Target's commitment to education extends to collaborations with other organizations to champion the cause of at-risk students and helping improve the graduation rate. Here, Target partnered with retired U.S. Army General and former Secretary of State Colin Powell, who is also the founding chairman of America's Promise Alliance, and his wife, Alma Powell, who is chair of the group's board. The Powells and Laysha, in her role as a Target executive, jointly authored an editorial that was published in the *Washington Post*, under the headline "At-risk students need more help from us, not Washington." The editorial cited findings from the "Don't Call Them Dropouts" report, which was based on a survey of 2,000 high-school age young people. This report, sponsored by Target, found that the reasons students leave school before graduating "are primarily environmental—including chronic absenteeism, home-lessness, unsafe neighborhoods, negative role models, and the need to be caregivers for parents and siblings."[7]

What these young people need, the editorial states, "is not necessarily more action in Washington but more action from us: caring adults willing to engage in a developmental relationship and the ability to help them imagine—and work toward—a better future." The higher proportion of African-American and Hispanic non-graduates translates into "more significant risk for the communities of color that will make up the U.S. majority by 2043. This is not a winning formula for the United States' future."[8]

[7] Colin L. Powell, Alma J. Powell, and Laysha Ward, "Opinions: At-Risk Students Need More Help from Us, Not Washington," *Washington Post*, August 29, 2014.
[8] Powell, Powell, and Ward, "Opinions."

My personal biases as a father of five and a professor at Northwestern University aside, it's hard to think of many worthier causes than education. No wonder, then, that Laysha describes Target's education initiatives as being "guest-centered." (A visit to a local Target on a weekend reveals families, many with young children, throughout the store. In late August, many of the shopping carts were filled with back-to-school supplies.)

Guests who know the extent of Target's commitment to furthering goals such as affordable education, supporting young learners, and raising the high school graduation rate are likely to be loyal to the retail chain. As Hessekiel noted, ". . . You can count on consumer participation if there's a worthy cause with a clearly articulated story to rally behind."[9]

Target also provides opportunities for consumers to participate in education initiatives. For example, Target enables guests to allocate 1 percent of the amounts spent on their Target credit cards and debit cards to any public or private K-12 school of their choice. What started as a pilot program is now in its 18th year. In this way, Target as a best citizen is making its customers into best partners in its philanthropic endeavors.

AN EMPOWERED TEAM

Too often social responsibility is a top-down exercise. The senior leaders decide where and how resources will be spent and which causes will be supported. A values-based leader, however, seeks to promote best citizenship by empowering the entire team to have a say in how the organization puts its values into action. In this way, best citizenship also supports having a best team, as people throughout the enterprise are encouraged to provide feedback and suggestions on philanthropic activities, such as they are in other endeavors.

---

[9] Hessekiel, "How Your Company Can Lead the Consumer Cause-Marketing Charge."

Some enterprises take it to the next level by taking a best-partner approach as well, asking for input from their customers on the issues that mean the most to them or that touch their lives every day.

Target Corporation has taken this integrated approach, especially in support of the number-one priority that resonates the strongest for their team members and customers alike: education. As an exemplary best citizen, Target put the resources of the organization and its teams to work for education, working from the grassroots up. In fact, the company encourages team members to become involved as volunteers in schools in their communities, which further aligns grassroots support with corporate initiatives.

"Team members are leading and serving . . . in the communities that they live and work in," Laysha says. This helps the company "attract people who are purpose driven. This inspires them to be part of a winning team like ours."

THE VALUES-BASED CULTURE

Best citizenship starts with self-reflection on the organizational level: Who are we and what do we stand for? Just as with best self, which happens through a continual process of *becoming* by increasing self-knowledge and self-awareness, best citizenship requires individuals and organizations to hold up a mirror to assess their commitments and actions. In addition to looking at what they're doing, these organizations need to continually evaluate why, to ensure authenticity and alignment with the communities in which they operate and with their important constituents, such as team members and customers.

At this point, best citizenship comes full circle, completing and enhancing the other four bests. Through best citizenship, organizations attract people who are becoming their best selves and willingly engage in creating best teams, not only in good times but also in challenging ones. Best citizenship elevates best partnerships, as parties hold each other accountable, with understanding and respect for what each party needs to be successful. Best investment produces the return that enables corporate social responsibility. Best citizenship creates alignment with the community in which the organization operates in the service of shared value.

With shared value, societal and economic progress become interconnected, touching issues such as food sourcing, natural resource usage, worker safety, health and well being, education and training, and environmental impact. Porter and Kramer challenge companies to apply the shared-value lens to their decision-making, so that societal benefits are present at the start, whether in the design of products or the impact of a new facility on a community. "If a company can improve societal conditions, it will often improve business conditions and thereby trigger positive feedback loops," the authors stated.[10]

All organizations leave a footprint everywhere they operate, from the facilities they build and the materials they source, to the people they train and develop. Best citizenship helps ensure that this footprint becomes a trail of good, aligned with and supportive of business objectives, for the benefit of all. Moreover, best citizenship marks a trail for other organizations as they undertake their own values-based leadership journey—doing well by doing good.

[10] Porter and Kramer, "Creating Shared Value."

CHAPTER 10

LIVING THE LEGACY AND LEAVING A GLOBAL FOOTPRINT

I t is one thing to talk about putting values into action to change the world, and quite another to see it firsthand. In the summer of 2014, as this book was being written, my family and I had the privilege of such an experience. We spent three weeks in Kenya, most of it in rural farming communities to witness the amazing transformation being brought about by One Acre Fund (www.OneAcreFund.org), a not-for-profit organization that was co-founded by Andrew Youn, a 2006 graduate of Northwestern University's Kellogg School of Management.

Although many professional opportunities, from Wall Street to management consulting, were available to Andrew, he took his MBA to the developing world—specifically, Kenya. He found the inspiration for his unusual path in mid-2005 when as an MBA intern in South Africa he took a side trip to Kenya. There, he met two farmers who were neighbors, but with completely different crop harvests. One was yielding two tons of food per acre, which enabled her to feed her children and provide a proper house for them. The other was harvesting only a quarter of that amount on the same size plot. The second farmer's children were thin and stunted in growth. She had also lost a child, which is all too common in an area of the world where the majority of childhood deaths are from hunger-related causes. The reason for this stark difference, Andrew discovered, was that the first farmer was using commercial seed and fertilizer, and planting and irrigating properly, while the second was not.

Closing that gap in agricultural supplies and techniques, Andrew concluded, would change the trajectory of the lives of rural farmers and their families, raising them out of poverty and ending the cycle of hunger. In 2006, Andrew launched a pilot project with 40 farmers in Kenya, providing access to seed, fertilizer, financing, and training in agricultural techniques. As of this writing in late 2014, One Acre Fund serves more than 200,000 farm families, touching more than 1 million people in Kenya and Rwanda, and expanding into Tanzania and several other African countries—doubling and tripling crop yields. Its goal is to serve 1 million farm families, which translates to more than 5 million people, by 2020. Moreover, the increases in these farmers' harvests will carry the additional compounded benefit of helping to feed an estimated 5 million more of their neighbors.

FARM FAMILIES SERVED PER YEAR BY ONE ACRE FUND

Although compelling, these numbers (see Figure 10.1) alone cannot tell the story in quite the same way as seeing One Acre Fund in action. Being an avid supporter and having followed Andrew Youn and One Acre Fund's tremendous successes for many years, I made the trip from Chicago to Kenya, along with my wife, Julie, and our three youngest children. I had seen the pictures, read the updates, and heard Andrew speak; therefore, I expected to be impressed and inspired. To say my expectations were exceeded on this trip, my first to Africa, is an understatement. We were simply blown away by the excitement, joy, and enthusiasm

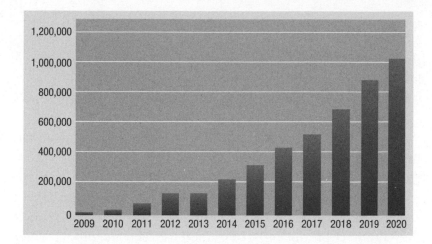

Figure 10.1   *As the number of farm families served grows, so does the reach of One Acre Fund, increasing productivity per acre and feeding more people.*
Source: One Acre Fund

being generated by One Acre Fund among the farmers it serves and empowers.

Visiting several of the One Acre Fund field sites in Kenya also brought me full circle. For the past 10 years, I have committed myself to making a difference by helping students and executives, alike, become values-based leaders. During that time, I met Andrew at Kellogg and heard about his passion for helping farmers in East Africa, who are among the approximately 1 billion people living on less than $1 a day. After that, I wanted to support him in any way I could. Since then this organization has been the recipient of the proceeds from the sale of this book and my previous work, *From Values to Action*, as well as speaking fees from my leadership presentations (more than 500 talks in four years, and counting).

Through my books and my talks on values-based leadership, I have raised money as well as awareness, which has helped spread the word about One Acre Fund. I truly believe that, when illustrating values-based leadership in action, Andrew and One Acre Fund are outstanding examples of becoming a best citizen.

PUTTING FARMERS FIRST

In the rural community of Bungoma, Kenya, which is about 300 miles northwest of Nairobi, we met a farmer who beamed as she explained that her one-acre plot now produces *five times* the yield she previously harvested before working with One Acre Fund. She produces more than enough to feed her family and, by selling the surplus, has purchased a cow and a goat, bought clothing for her family, and constructed a modest home. This farmer's pride was tangible proof of One Acre's vision, as stated on its web site: "When farmers improve their harvests, they pull themselves out of poverty. They also start producing surplus food for their neighbors. When farmers prosper, they eradicate poverty and hunger in their communities."[1]

Touring the farms and fields, I was amazed at how eager the farmers were to show us their crops and livestock and to have us meet their families and children. These people work very hard—planting, cultivating, and harvesting under the hot sun—but they are achieving significant results for themselves and their families. The direct connection between the size of the harvest and health of a community was obvious, even to an outside observer. The farmers who partner with One Acre Fund put faces on these success stories. Several years ago, before signing up with One Acre Fund, Patrick was a subsistence farmer who, despite his efforts, could not provide enough for his family. In the months immediately following a harvest, there was food to eat, but as time went on, supplies dwindled and eventually Patrick and his family ran out of food. This marked the start of the "hunger season" when the previous harvest was exhausted but new crops had not yet matured. When we met Patrick in Bungoma, he had been part of One Acre Fund for eight years, and is now working as a farm manager for the organization, which employs and trains local people for various positions, from field

[1] One Acre Fund, "Vision," OneAcreFund.org web site, 2014.

officers and farm managers to senior directors. Working on his laptop, Patrick kept track of hundreds of farm families, recording their crop yields and the status of their loan payments.

These success stories offer hope against a backdrop that tells a sad truth about too many farmers in Africa, who are among the world's poor. As Roger Thurow writes in his book, *The Last Hunger Season*, which profiles the success of One Acre Fund, the concept of "hungry farmers" is one of the "most confounding, troubling phrases on a confounding, troubled continent. . . . How can farmers, who rise every morning to grow food, be hungry?"[2]

Since 2006, One Acre Fund has sought to change that sad truth, with amazing and inspiring successes in communities, where farmers are able to grow enough to feed their families and to sell the surplus. Furthermore, by tapping their potential in other ways, people who had been subsistence farmers are becoming business owners, employing others and earning the respect in their communities from neighbors who now see them as leaders. Eradicating poverty and raising the standard of living empowers the next generation, as children are educated and can go on to realize their potential of becoming teachers, doctors, and business people. The benefits from becoming a best citizen compound throughout a community and beyond, to improve the standard of living within a country and around the world.

THE ETHOS OF GIVING

As stated in Chapter 9, for-profit organizations that are committed to being best citizens typically become involved in philanthropy locally, nationally, and even internationally, such as through a foundation or by providing funding and grants. These best citizen-companies believe that, first and foremost, it is the right thing to do,

[2] Roger Thurow, *The Last Hunger Season: A Year in an African Farm Community on the Brink of Change* (New York: Public Affairs, 2012).

while also fostering a positive connection with team members, partners, customers, and other stakeholders, as with the example of Target Corporation.

What makes One Acre Fund unique is that being a best citizen is not a sideline. Its core mission and vision is to serve poor, rural farmers in Africa; that is the sole reason why the organization exists. Andrew refers to this vision as the "ethos of becoming a best citizen," the belief that "we are here to improve as many lives as possible." He further explains, "This is our purpose and our meaning, as it is for many people in the world. What brings meaning to our lives is enabling other people to reach their potential."[3]

Before founding One Acre Fund, Andrew considered a number of opportunities for what he called a "mission-oriented career," including working for a large nonprofit organization. "But I became obsessed with the idea" of helping African farmers become more productive, Andrew says, even though he admittedly knew nothing about farming at the time. "Any kind of entrepreneurial activity requires some irrationality," he adds with a laugh.

With a pilot project involving 40 farmers, Andrew demonstrated a simple but dramatic model that proved the value of using commercial seed and fertilizer, and the benefits of proper planting. "The farmers' wild success, even though I knew nothing about farming, gave me the confidence to go forward," he says.

The ethos of giving that Andrew describes should not be confused with giving handouts. This giving is in the form of training and service, to empower the farmers so that they can become more productive, reap larger harvests, and realize better prices in the market. It is the adage of teaching a man to fish in action. "Everything we do is for the betterment of community and society. To me, the best way to accomplish that is by empowering people," Andrew says. "Every person has incredible potential. However, billions of

---

[3] Andrew Youn, telephone interview, August 29, 2014. Quotes and data regarding One Acre Fund come from this interview unless otherwise indicated.

people on the planet never have the opportunity to reach a fraction of that potential. That's horrifying! Helping people to tap their potential is an incredibly beautiful thing when it happens."

While such endeavors are noble-minded, Andrew also called them "selfish" in so far as the person who is the benefactor is also a beneficiary. Those who do good also derive incredible meaning and a sense of purpose from empowering others. "It enriches us, too, as we work together to help others achieve that potential," he adds.

FINDING MEANING

There might be a temptation to romanticize an organization like One Acre Fund, seeing it as an inspiring example of what some mission-driven people (*those guys* with a purpose) are doing in the world. While that is absolutely true, if we stop there, we do ourselves, our communities, and even the world at large a huge disservice.

Becoming a best citizen, like all facets of values-based leadership, speaks to a deep human desire within all people to find meaning in what we do. Being a best citizen is not just a nice idea that makes the workplace more team-friendly or elevates the organization's rankings on those lists of the best places to work. It is absolutely essential.

Without meaning, work becomes a series of tasks with no urgency or importance attached to them. Already in this book, we have seen examples of how organizations are infusing meaning into the work of their teams, such as Edwards Lifesciences Corporation, which invites patients who have received its heart valves to visit its manufacturing facility. When people discover a deeper, broader meaning in what they do, they are highly motivated to do even more. "When people see that they are making a meaningful contribution to the world, that helps them become more engaged in their day-to-day work," Andrew remarks.

As team members develop personally and professionally to more fully realize their potential (as we discussed in Section Two on best teams), people are empowered and equipped to take on greater responsibility. Team members actively seek out more opportunities to elevate their day-to-day responsibilities with meaning, significance, and excellence. With best citizenship, the values-based culture goes to the next level, from developing the internal team to helping people elsewhere to realize their potential.

THE ONE ACRE MODEL

It was a Monday, and, as in organizations everywhere, time for a team meeting. The leader was tracking results and talking to the team about accountability—the kinds of activities you'd probably find at a tech firm in Silicon Valley, a health-care company in the American Midwest, or a financial firm in New York. On this particular Monday, however, I was sitting in on a One Acre Fund team meeting in Bungoma, Kenya, where a farm manager was stressing the importance of farmers repaying their loans, so that more people could borrow to purchase the commercial seed and fertilizer they needed to improve their productivity. Here was the One Acre model in action; what the organization describes as a "business solution for smallholder farmers" (individuals who run a small subsistence farm with a mixture of cash crops).

"We see the farmers as our customers. That means we work for *them*, providing the services that they demand," Andrew explains. "The farmer is our boss."

The One Acre Fund model follows four steps. The first is the distribution of seed and fertilizer. In rural areas such as Bungoma, there is no easy access to basic supplies and technology. To bring the supplies within reach of the farmers, One Acre hires hundreds of trucks to distribute tens of thousands of tons of supplies to more than 1,000 distribution points in rural areas. At each of those distribution points, 100 to 200 farmers gather to pick up their supplies and then carry them back on foot to their plots of land. Without facilitating local access of basic agricultural supplies, One Acre Fund could not work at the grassroots level.

The second step is providing financing that enables farmers to purchase the seed and fertilizer they need. The typical loan transaction is $80. What would constitute a microloan by Western standards or a tiny transaction that most of us would not think twice about (indeed, my coffee-drinking friends are known to load their Starbucks cards with nearly that much), is a major financial commitment for these rural farmers.

Along with the financing comes the education of how the process works: The loan must be paid back so that the money can be recycled to help more farmers. Over the course of the nine-month term of the loans, the money trickles in—$2 here, $10 there. "It's usually a few wrinkled bills," Andrew says. Using a paper-based accounting system, the loan payments are recorded in ledgers. "Ninety-nine percent of our farmers pay on time," he adds, which is powerful testimony of the pride farmers feel in being self-sufficient.

The third part of the model is training in agricultural techniques, which is handled by a dedicated team that studies what works best for crops in a particular area, and then translates those steps for rural farmers. "Some of the most important techniques are remarkably simple, such as using a planting string [marked at intervals] to show how to space the seed so that each plant gets the same amount of water and light," Andrew explains. "Another example is using about a thimbleful of fertilizer in each planting hole so that it goes to the plant, and doesn't run off into the environment."

Farmers gather every week in groups of about 30 to attend training sessions. The format is a short discussion to explain the technique, followed by the main event—going out in the fields so farmers can practice what they have just learned. Having witnessed these sessions, I can attest that any organization wanting to establish a culture of continuous learning could glean important lessons from One Acre Fund and the knowledge-hungry farmers it serves.

The fourth and last step in the model is what One Acre calls "market facilitation," enabling farmers to maximize their profits from harvest sales. The farmers primarily grow basic staple foods, such as grains, which are bought by middlemen, who typically aggregate small purchases into larger quantities. Often, in this scenario, "the farmer gets a pretty bad deal," Andrew says, because the amounts being sold in each transaction are so small.

One Acre Fund increases the farmers' market power with middlemen by negotiating on behalf of 100 or so farmers at one time. The entire process becomes more efficient and fair for all parties: The farmers get a better deal and the middlemen are able to buy larger quantities at once, which saves them a lot of time.

While these steps may seem simple, that's what makes them powerful and replicable. Too often, in organizations everywhere, people like to make things unnecessarily complicated. The solutions that work best are generally those that are fairly simple. Solutions, however, cannot be dictated in a vacuum. They must be developed and adapted by spending time "on the ground" talking to people about what works and doesn't work—whether walking around a factory floor or going out into the cornfields in Kenya.

LESSONS LEARNED FROM A KENYAN FARM FIELD

It's a rare treat to observe the growth of a best-citizen organization from the ground up. In less than a decade, One Acre Fund has gone from being a small seed of an idea to an internationally acclaimed organization that receives support and funding from a variety of sources, including:

- **The Bill & Melinda Gates Foundation**, which in November 2013 launched a three-year, $11.6 million partnership to leverage the One Acre Fund operating model to bring innovative agriculture technologies to more rural farm families.

- **MasterCard Foundation**, which in October 2013 announced a $10 million partnership that expands access to financial services and training for smallholder farmers in Kenya, Rwanda, and Burundi. The partnership will enable One Acre Fund to serve more rural smallholder farmers, and employ more than 770 additional staff members. The partnership is linked to Kenya's microfinance sector as well, aiming to increase the availability of such lending in rural Africa.
- **Schwab Foundation**, which in 2013 presented its Social Entrepreneur Award to One Acre Fund. The foundation collaborated with the World Economic Forum to recognize Andrew Youn, among others, for their innovative global contributions.
- **The Barr Foundation**, which pledged an additional $3.7 million (following about $1 million in earlier grants) through 2016 to support crop insurance, tree planting, solar lights, and staple crop diversification.
- **USAID**, which awarded a total of $3.5 million in grants between 2012 and 2014.

Although One Acre Fund was founded with enthusiasm and clarity of purpose to help rural farmers, like any new organization it endured its share of failures while refining its model. "We've had many failures and lessons learned," Andrew admits. In fact, failure, itself, is one of the lessons learned. "Establishing a culture that tolerates failure is very important," he adds.

Among those early failures, Andrew explains, were attempts to "impose too many of my own beliefs onto our farmers—such as growing fancy, high-value crops—without listening to my customers. It was a 'my idea-driven' failure." Fortunately, it happened early on, before One Acre tried to scale its growth. The lesson here is "to fail small and quickly," Andrew adds. "Since that experience we have learned to listen to our customers much better, and to elevate them so that we see them as our bosses."

Andrew's candor about initial failures and subsequent adjustments underscores the importance of the servant leader. Whether at the top of a large for-profit company or a philanthropic organization, the servant leader seeks first to understand the needs of others, specifically customers and the valued team members who serve and support them. Servant leaders are not interested in pushing their own ideas, but rather want to embrace others' ideas, based on their culture, history, priorities, and beliefs, and implement the best overall solution. "When someone is trying to do good in the world, there is often this attitude of, 'Hey, I'm doing good and people should be grateful.' They have forgotten to listen, and to treat others like they are customers," Andrew says. "The question is, 'What is my role in getting them what they need?' not 'How do I deliver my idea?'"

Andrew's observation reminded me of an experience I had as CEO of Baxter International when I attended the World Economic Forum in Davos, Switzerland. Gathered at the forum were leaders from around the world, many of whom were genuinely interested in tackling the major issues on our planet, from poverty and malnutrition to health care, education, and environmental protection. One evening at dinner, two Americans were being honored for contributing millions of dollars to fund an HIV/AIDS program in Africa. As I listened to the speeches, I was very inspired by how wonderful this initiative was, until the woman next to me spoke up. She was a health minister from an African country with a different perspective: As she saw it, AIDS, while a serious threat, was not the only health crisis on the continent that deserved attention. Access to clean water and malaria prevention also remained serious and urgent problems. Her comments have always stayed with me because they highlight the importance of working with a particular community, country, or region to identify their priorities first, before deciding where to channel resources.

The Gates Foundation, for example, has focused much of its health-related initiatives on infectious diseases affecting more than

1 billion people in developing countries—serious illnesses that, as the foundation states, "attract little donor funding, largely because those diseases are rare in wealthier countries." One such disease that has been all but defeated is *dracunculiasis* (guinea worm disease), with only 541 reported cases in 2012. The Gates Foundation is also part of a public–private partnership (along with 13 pharmaceutical companies; the United States, the United Kingdom, and the United Arab Emirates; the World Bank; and other global health organizations) to "control or eliminate 10 neglected tropical diseases by the end of the decade."[4]

Here we are reminded of the importance of genuine humility: The best-citizen organization seeks first to understand others before deciding how best to help them.

THE FIVE BESTS IN ACTION

As the fifth in the series of *bests*, it is no surprise that to be a best citizen, an organization or individual must rely on the other four bests. It starts with the best self, understanding what one's values are and using the four principles of values-based leadership—self-reflection, balance and perspective, true self-confidence, and genuine humility—to identify and commit to what matters most. From the earliest stages of One Acre Fund, Andrew acted as his best self when he committed to becoming a mission-driven person and to use his knowledge, education, and other resources to tackle problems as huge and daunting as poverty and hunger, one family farm at a time.

For each of us, no matter how great or limited our abilities and resources might be, we, too, start with becoming our best selves. Through self-reflection and with greater self-awareness, we are guided to what we can do, how we can do it, and our motivations

---

[4]The Gates Foundation, "Neglected Infectious Diseases," Gates Foundation web site, 2014. www.gatesfoundation.org/What-We-Do/Global-Health/Neglected-Infectious-Diseases.

for doing so. At every phase, our ongoing commitment to be our best self helps keep us on track.

No mission, commercial or philanthropic, can be accomplished on our own. A best team must be developed and put in place. At One Acre Fund, we found evidence of best teams everywhere, such as the recruits from Harvard, Stanford, the University of Virginia, and other universities who, like Andrew, put their education to work in the farm fields of rural Africa. Other valued team members include local talent, many of whom are former subsistence farmers, who have become farm managers earning a salary from One Acre Fund. (To date, One Acre Fund has hired 1,800 people.) With its best team, One Acre Fund is committed to "growing as quickly as humanly possible," Andrew explains. "We have set this ambitious goal for ourselves because of the unbelievable need that exists in the world."

Best partnerships allow products and ideas to flow up and down the supply chain. In the case of One Acre Fund, a strong partnership must be created with farmers, who are the customers. Without their commitment, One Acre Fund cannot carry out its mission. In addition, One Acre Fund develops partnerships in other areas of the supply chain, from distribution of supplies to marketing the end products.

Being a best investment, an organization generates a return for the money invested by stakeholders. One Acre Fund shows its strength as a best investment by turning donations into tangible help for farmers to end the cycle of hunger and poverty. As a supporter, I am also an investor in One Acre Fund, and I was very moved by the *return* my dollars generated in Bungoma. Like many best-citizen investments, this return was not visible in my bank account, but rather in the prosperous and enthusiastic farmers who are now able to send their healthy children to school.

This brings us to the heart of a best citizen, where there is a commitment to making the world a better place. Here is values-based leadership in action for the greatest and broadest benefit: to help others to reach their full potential. For some people, values-based leadership will take them far afield, changing the world in dramatic ways, as One Acre Fund has done for Andrew. Others may become involved closer to home, within their own communities. There is no hierarchy on the scale of doing good works.

Some individuals and organizations are best citizens in their local communities where they can make a difference. Others take best citizenship to the next level by becoming citizens of the world, focused on the commonalities among all humans, instead of the differences. To illustrate, incoming MBA students at Kellogg fill out a survey asking them what they value and what they wish for the world. During their first week of studies, the students get to see a list of their classmates' answers. Incredibly, this diverse group from all backgrounds and parts of the world share many of the same priorities—world peace, happiness, the importance of family, etc.—and similar aspirations. These students, arguably among the best and brightest, are best citizens in the making. The more this happens and the more we truly understand each other, the closer the world comes together.

Each of us, no matter our experience level or resources, can begin today, right where we are. It starts with the five bests, the foundation of which is becoming your best self. This growth journey begins with self-reflection to discover your values and priorities, goals and desires. *What is my life purpose? What matters most? Where can I make a difference? How can I reach my full potential?* Becoming one's best self is a never-ending process, and continuously reorients us to our values and goals. Even in every other best stage—team, partner, investment, and citizen—we are always becoming our best selves.

The continuous, self-reflective nature of values-based leadership makes it a journey. Therefore, you might think of the five bests as the roadmap for where it might take you. Whatever you do and wherever you go, you will not be alone. Other values-based leaders are out there and many more are being inspired by the example of people like Andrew Youn and the work of One Acre Fund. As a values-based leader, by developing the fullness of your potential through the five bests, there is no limit to the good you can do in your life, your community, your country, and the world.

ACKNOWLEDGMENTS

G iven the large number of people who have influenced my beliefs about values-based leadership, I find it challenging to keep this section brief.

My late parents, Harry and Patricia Kraemer, gave me a strong foundation of values. They both passed away within the past few years, but they are never far from my thoughts or those of my wonderful siblings, Steve, Paul, Marilyn, and Tommy.

I am forever in debt to Julie, my wife of 35 years. While I often say that together we manage five fantastic children (Suzie, Andrew, Shannon, Diane, and Daniel), Julie sometimes teases me that she is a single parent managing *six* children, with a large age spread between me and the other five.

I was extremely fortunate to work with an amazing group of leaders from the former Baxter Travenol and American Hospital Supply as they came together to form Baxter International. I learned much from these leaders, as well as from my colleagues at businesses that were spun off from Baxter, including Caremark, Allegiance, and Edwards Lifesciences.

I have been truly blessed to have the opportunity to teach alongside outstanding professors at Northwestern University's Kellogg School of Management. Deans Donald Jacobs, Dipak Jain, and Sally Blount have been extremely supportive of my teaching and writing. A special acknowledgment goes to my phenomenal Kellogg students who teach me as much as I teach them. I often say that I never truly understand a topic until I can explain it clearly to a group of bright, energetic people.

In addition, I want to thank:

Dev Patel, Khalid Ali, and Debbie Brauer who encouraged me to take values-based leadership to the next level—both on the road and in this second book.

At Madison Dearborn Partners, all of my colleagues, including Tim Sullivan, Nick Alexos, Paul Finnegan, Sam Mencoff, and John Canning, who have provided me with many examples of leadership across MDP's entire investment portfolio.

All of the management teams and board members with whom I am honored to work at Leidos Corporation, Science Application International, Catamaran Corporation, Sirona Dental, VWR International, Sage Products, Ikaria Corporation, Northwestern University, Kellogg School of Management, Lawrence University of Wisconsin, NorthShore University Healthsystem, The Conference Board, and the Archdiocese of Chicago Catholic Schools. Through these organizations, I have been fortunate to be exposed to a variety of excellent values-based leaders.

This book would not be possible without several outstanding values-based leaders who shared their wisdom and insights on the *five bests*. Their enthusiasm for the topic and willingness to share their experiences speaks volumes about their commitment to values-based leadership and to serve as role models for others. My deepest thanks to those profiled in these chapters: Doug Conant, former president and CEO, Campbell Soup Company; Gary Gorman, founder and president, Gorman & Co. Inc.; Kelly Grier, vice chair, talent, Ernst & Young Americas; Mark Neaman, president and CEO, NorthShore University HealthSystem; Jai Shekhawat, CEO and founder, Fieldglass; Tim Sullivan, managing director, Madison Dearborn Partners; Mark Thierer, chairman & CEO, Catamaran Corporation; Rick Waddell, chairman and CEO, Northern Trust; Laysha Ward, president, community relations, Target Corporation; and Andrew Youn, co-founder, One Acre Fund.

I also want to thank my editors at Jossey-Bass, Karen Murphy and Judy Howarth, for their enthusiasm for this project.

I am deeply grateful to Khalid Ali, a former student and a 2014 graduate of Kellogg, for his constant encouragement and challenges each step of the way, which helped make this a better book.

Thank you to the many colleagues, students, and friends who took the time to read drafts of this book, including Tim Sullivan, Raul Trillo, Samir Gokhale, Dev Patel, Steve Meyer, Maureen Meyer, Debbie Brauer, Paige Kobele, Daven Morrison, and Ben Zastawny.

And finally, a very special thanks to Tricia Crisafulli, my collaborator, counselor, friend, and colleague, for her efforts. Without Tricia, as a best partner, this book would not be possible. Thank you, Tricia!

Harry M. Jansen Kraemer Jr.
Wilmette, Illinois

Harry M. Jansen Kraemer Jr. is a professor of management and strategy at Northwestern University's Kellogg School of Management, where he teaches in the MBA and Executive MBA programs. He is also an executive partner with Madison Dearborn Partners, one of the leading private equity firms in the United States, where he consults with CEOs and other top executives of companies in Madison Dearborn's extensive portfolio. Kraemer is the former chairman and CEO of Baxter International Inc., a multibillion-dollar global health-care company, and serves on the boards of several public, private, and not-for-profit organizations. He graduated *summa cum laude* from Lawrence University in Wisconsin in 1977 and received an MBA degree from the Kellogg School of Management in 1979. A recognized expert in values-based leadership, Kraemer is the author of the best-selling *From Values to Action: The Four Principles of Values-Based Leadership* (Jossey-Bass, 2011), and speaks widely on the topic. He was also featured in *Comebacks* (Jossey-Bass, 2010), a collection of leadership profiles. He was voted the Kellogg School Professor of the Year in 2008.

Harry, his wife, Julie, and their five children live in Wilmette, Illinois.

For more information and to read Harry's blog, please visit http://harrykraemer.org/.

Accidents, self-reflection and, 24
Accountability:
 One Acre model and, 192
 organizational, 131
 ownership mentality of, 165
Acquisitions:
 best-partner approach and reduced risk
  with, 127
 of best partners, 95, 123–127
 failed, 124
 integration after, 86, 163
 pursuing external growth through,
  57, 58
 self-reflection and, 125, 126
 stock prices and, 163
 that take too long to integrate, 59
 warning signs with, 126
Admitting when you are wrong, true
  self-confidence and, 39–40
African-American students, graduation rate
  for, 181
Agricultural training, One Acre model and,
  193
AIDS, 196
AIG. See American International Group
Alignment, authenticity and creation of,
  176–177, 183
Allstate, 87
Alpha:
 total shareholder return and, 153
 values-based leadership and, 164
ALS. See Amyotrophic lateral sclerosis
Amazon, 73, 162
American College of Healthcare
  Executives, 103
American International Group, 87
America's Promise Alliance, GradNation
  program, 181
Amyotrophic lateral sclerosis, Ice Bucket
  Challenge and, 177
Answers, opinions vs., 29

Anxiety:
 eliminating, 20–23
 lack of self-reflection and, 28
Apple, 73
Apprenticeship model, talent development
  and, 144
Attitude:
 emotional bank account of organization
  and, 66
 ownership in start-ups and, 84
Authenticity:
 alignment and, 176–177, 183
 true self-confidence, genuine humility,
  and, 33
Autonomy, Hewlett-Packard's acquisition
  of, 57

Bad times, balancing, 22
Balance, 1, 3, 5, 13, 41, 65, 167. See also
  Perspective
 in action, 197
 best citizenship and, 180
 best investments and, 133
 best partners and, 92
 best teams and, 49
 culture and, 145
 customer best partnerships and, 115
 employing, values-based leaders and, 48
 self-reflection and, 28–30, 31–32
 start-up companies and, 83
 talent development and, 138
 turnaround leaders and, 71
Balanced individuals, best self, self-
  reflection, and, 30–31
Bank of America, 74
Banks, interest rate environment and, 156–157
Barr Foundation, 195
Baxter International, 3, 4, 12, 88, 113, 115,
  142, 147, 148, 149, 160, 161, 172
 Custom Sterile line, 116–117
 Value Link Program, 116

Bear Stearns, 155
Best citizens/best citizenship, 6, 8, 167–169.
    See also One Acre Fund
  authenticity, creation of alignment and,
    176–177
  becoming, 176
  best self integrated into, 172
  empowered teams and, 182–183
  finding meaning in what you do and,
    191–192
  five bests in action and, 197–199
  holistic perspective on, 171–172
  meaning of, 167
  optimal footprint with, 184
  shift in thinking around, 173–176
  social responsibility and, 174
  Target Corporation's philanthropic
    initiatives and, 172, 178–182
  total shareholder return and, 153
  values-based culture and, 183–184
  values-based leadership in action and,
    198–199
  values in action and, 171–184
Best investments, 6, 7, 8, 131–133, 171
  in action, 198
  becoming, 157–160
  corporate social responsibility and, 184
  disruptive technology and, 165
  "5 Cs" of, 164–165
  genuine humility and, 166
  holistic approach to, 133, 157, 162
  incentives tied to becoming, 160–163
  "industry, company, management, and
    deal" criteria for, 165–166
  "people agenda" and, 139–140
  prerequisites of, 136–137
  self-reflection and, 166
  socially responsible activities and, 175
  in talent, 135–150
  talent and culture and, 140–141
  talent development for, 144–146
  team-mindset and, 147–150
  testing, 166
  total shareholder return and, 153
Best partners/best partnerships, 6, 7, 131,
    133. *See also* Customer best partnership;
    Suppliers as best partners
  acquisitions and, 95, 123–127
  in action, 198
  best citizenship and, 176, 183–184
  best investments and, 164, 171
  best teams intersecting with, 105, 108
  Catamaran and Cigna win and, 128–129
  Catamaran Corporation success story,
    118–123
  communication skills and, 93–94

competitive pressures and, 99–100
  discernment and, 101
  end users and, 129
  global initiatives and, 169
  holistic approach with, 93
  innovation and, 121–123
  long-term, earning, 100–102
  mutual successes and, 95
  organizations and, 91–92
  in strategic, long-term arrangements, 94
  total shareholder return and, 153
  values-based leadership and, 92
Best self, 5, 131, 133, 167
  best citizenship and, 172
  best team based on, 49
  centering, 23–24
  continual process of becoming, 183
  entrepreneurs and, 75
  every day, 32
  ongoing commitment to, 12, 197–198
  in real world, 24–25
  self-reflection and responding to, 21
  total shareholder return and, 153
  turnaround of company and, 71
  values-based leadership and, 11
Best teams, 6, 7, 49–53, 68, 131, 133
  in action, 198
  aligned with founder's values, 76–77
  best citizenship and, 176
  best investments and, 171
  best partners intersecting with, 105, 108
  Campbell Soup Company turnaround
    and, 68
  at Catamaran Corporation, 122
  characteristics of, 50–51
  core values of start-ups and, 74–77
  creating, 49–50
  essence of, 62
  feedback and, 51, 58, 85
  at Fieldglass, 77–88
  form, storm, norm, and perform concept
    and, 62–63
  growth in start-up companies and, 82
  leaders unequipped for, 56
  leader-team engagement and, 65
  at NorthShore University HealthSystem,
    105, 106
  out-of-the-box thinking and, 84–85
  ownership in start-ups and, 84
  rewarding, 87–88
  start-up companies and, 88–89
  success and, 53
  talent and, 164
  total shareholder return and, 153
  traits not needed in, 50
  turnaround leaders and, 71

Bill & Melinda Gates Foundation, 194, 196, 197
Boeing's 787 Dreamliner, 107
Bosses, leading up and, 25–27
Boston College Center for Corporate Citizenship, Campbell Soup Company turnaround and, 69
Bottom-line growth, 136
Broken organizations, causes of, 56–57
Burundi, One Acre Fund and farm families in, 195
Business orientation of leadership, self-reflection and, 19–20

Calmness, daily self-reflection and, 27
Campbell Soup Company, 52
    Douglas Campbell and turnaround at, 60–70
    employee engagement ratio at, 61, 68
    employee engagement turn around at, 63–66
    form, storm, norm, and perform concept at, 62–63
    inside turnaround at, 67–68
    price increases and challenges faced by, 60–61
    winning in workplace, marketplace, and community at, 69–70
    winning on four dimensions at, 66–70
Capital expenditures, cash flow and, 158
Cardinal Health, NorthShore University HealthSystem partnership with, 110
Caremark Rx, 120
Carnegie, Andrew, 136
Cash flow:
    Campbell Soup Company turnaround and, 68
    on net present-value basis, stock prices and, 162–163
    shareholder return and, 158
Catalyst Award, Campbell Soup Company as recipient of, 69
Catalyst Health Solutions, SXC merger with, 120, 127, 128. See also Catamaran Corporation
Catamaran Corporation, 79, 95, 114
    best partnerships and growth of, 118–123
    business model snapshot for, 120–121
    as leading provider of PBM services, 118, 120, 121, 123
CEOs of start-ups, sound business ideas and, 82–83
Challenging each other, best teams and, 58, 84
Champy, Jim, 63
Character, best team and, 62

Chief engagement officer, CEO as, 65–66
Christopherson, Wes, 44, 45, 160
Cigna Corporation, Catamaran and best-partnership model with, 128–129
Collins, Jim, 58
Commitment, emotional bank account of organization and, 66
Communication:
    best investments and, 164
    best partnerships and, 93–94
    best teams and, 51–52
Community social agenda, Campbell Soup Company turnaround and, 69–70
Compaq Computer, 57
Compassion, best investment and, 164
Competence:
    best investments and, 164
    best teams and, 62
Competition, teams and, 50
Competitive advantage:
    best partners and, 98
    start-up companies and, 97–98
Competitive pressures, partnerships and response to, 99–100
Conant, Douglas, 52, 60–70
Confidence, true. See True confidence
Consistency, values-based organizations and, 61
Corporate Responsibility magazine, 69
Corporate social responsibility, 175, 184
Courage, best investment and, 164
Covington Capital Partners, 122
Crain's Chicago Business, 86
Credit market, financial crisis of 2008-2009 and, 155
Crises:
    self-reflection and, 22, 24
    team members, your best self, and, 24–25
Criticism from activist groups, depleting emotional bank account of organization and, 66
CRM. See Customer relationship management
Cross-borders mergers, 125
Cultural diversity, at Ernst & Young, 145
Culture:
    best investments and, 164
    broken organizations and shifts in, 56
    employees out of sync with, 141–144
    talent and, 140–145
Customer best partnership, what it is and isn't, 114–115
Customer orientation, best partnerships and, 98
Customer perspective, long-term best partnerships and, 101

Customer relationship management, 114
Customers:
  Campbell Soup Company turnaround and, 67
  types of, 113
Customer satisfaction, 114
CVS Caremark, 120

DaimlerChrysler merger, acquisition culture clash and, 125
Deaths, self-reflection and, 24
Dell, 73
Disappointments, groundedness in reality and, 22
Discernment:
  best citizenship and, 177
  best partnerships and, 101
  leading up and, 25
Disgruntled employees, depleting emotional bank account of organization and, 66
Disruptive technology, best investments and, 165
Disruptors, 73
Diverse opinions, gathering, 30
Dividends, shareholder, 152
Do the best you can, 22
Do the right thing, 22
Dow Jones Sustainability Index (North America), Campbell Soup Company and, 69
Dow Jones Sustainability World Index, Campbell Soup Company and, 69
Downsizing, 135
Dreamliner (Boeing), 107
Due diligence, acquisitions and, 124
Dysfunctional cultures, 57

Earnings per share gains, Campbell Soup Company turnaround and, 68
Economic progress, shared value and, 184
Education:
  shared value and, 184
  Target Corporation's commitment to, 180–182
Edwards Lifesciences Corporation, human connection and, 117–118, 191
Ego, best teams and subordination of, 80–81, 83
Electronic health records, 104
Electronic medical records, NorthShore-Epic systems collaboration and, 104, 105, 106, 107, 109, 110
Emotional bank account of organization, building, 66
Emotional intelligence, 26, 146

Employee engagement, Campbell Soup Company turnaround and, 63–66, 67
Employee stock ownership plan (ESOP), 160–161
Employee validation, emotional bank account of organization and, 66
Empowered teams, social responsibility and, 182–183
EMRs. *See* Electronic medical records
Endowment funds, 132, 163
Entrepreneurial field, growth in, 74
Entrepreneurs:
  best self and, 75
  genuine humility and, 81
  true self-confidence and, 81
Environment, shared value and, 184
Epic Systems Corporation, NorthShore University HealthSystem collaboration with, 104–106, 109, 110
Ernst & Young Americas, 133
  Operating Executive Committee, 138
  priority setting and, 137
Ernst & Young (EY), 77
  Americas Advisory Council, 139–140
  Global Advisory Council, 140
  "intellectual-agility" approach to talent development at, 146–147
  "people agenda" set at, 139–140
  quantitative targets and measures at, 138
  talent development at, 137, 144–146
Ernst & Young LLP, 139
ESOP. *See also* Employee stock ownership plan
Ethical behavior, emotional bank account of organization and, 66
Ethical issues, 8
Ethisphere magazine, Campbell Soup Company ethics cited by, 69–70
Excellence, best partners and pursuit of, 111
Exercise, scheduling and prioritizing, 30–31
Expansion phase, broken organizations and scenarios during, 56
EY Global Talent Executive Committee, 138

Facebook, 73, 162
Failed acquisitions, economics confused with strategy and, 124–125
Failure:
  self-reflection and, 24
  true self-confidence and learning from, 41
Fallibility, admitting, 39–40
False confidence, 36, 72
Farm families in East Africa, One Acre Fund and, 185–198

Fear:
  eliminating, 20–23
  lack of self-reflection and, 28
Feedback:
  best teams and, 51, 58, 85
  self-reflection and, 20, 32
Feed forward concept, in start-ups, 85
Fieldglass, 19, 20, 53, 74
  best team concept at, 77–88
  from launch to scale at, 82–84
  pre-mortem at, 85–86
  rewards for best team at, 87–88
  SAP purchase of, 20, 77, 78, 86, 88
  team building at, 78–79
  team first, ego last at, 80–81, 83
Financial crisis of 2008-2009:
  credit market freeze and, 155
  Gorman & Co. Inc. during, 75
Financial performance:
  benchmark analysis of, 152–153
  talent linked to, 150
Financial Times, 60, 63
Followership, leadership and, 36
Food drives, 177
Food sourcing, shared value and, 184
Forbes, 177
Ford Motor Company, 73
Form, storm, norm, and perform concept,
    best team at Campbell Soup Company
    and, 62–63
For-profit organizations, best citizenship
    and, 174
Fortune, 120
Foundations, best investments and, 132
Friedman, Milton, 173
Fundraising, peer-to-peer marketing and,
    177

Gallup Organization, 61, 68
General Electric, 74, 155
Genuine humility, 1, 3, 5, 7, 9, 13, 14, 33, 39,
    41, 98, 167, 180
  in action, 197
  best-citizen organizations and, 197
  best investments and, 166
  best partners and, 92
  best teams and, 50
  CEO of start-ups and, 83
  entrepreneurship and, 81
  in real world, 47–48
  respect and, 42
  turnaround leaders and, 71
  values-based leaders and, 11, 48
GlaxoSmithKline, 87
Global initiatives, best partners and, 169
Global logistics, cash flow and, 158

Global mindset, at Ernst & Young, 145
Gokhale, Samir, 4
Good times, managing, 22
Good to Great (Collins), 58
Goodwill, 177
Google, 73
Gorman, Gary, 75
Gorman & Co., Inc. (Wisconsin), 75
GPOs. See Group purchasing organizations
GradNation program (America's Promise
    Alliance), 181
Graduation rate, minority students and, 181
Graham, William B., 147, 172
Grier, Kelly, 133, 137, 138, 139, 140, 143,
    144, 145, 146, 147
Group purchasing organizations, 118
Growth:
  top- and bottom-line, 136
  types of, 123
Guinea worm disease (dracunculiasis), 197

Halo effect, corporate challenges and, 177
Hard work, success and factors beyond, 45,
    46
Health, shared value and, 184
Health care industry, dramatic changes in,
    102–103
Health information technology, 103
Health plan costs, Catamaran Corporation
    business model and, 121
"Hedghog concept," good-to-great
    companies and, 58
Hessekiel, David, 177
Hewlett-Packard, culture shift and failed
    leadership at, 57
HIMSS/Modern Healthcare, 103
Hiring:
  best teams for start-ups, 79–80, 88
  for leadership team, 122
  start-up success and, 83
Hispanic students, graduation rate for, 181
Human capital. See Talent
Human element, supply chain and,
    117–118
Human resources, cash flow, stock price,
    and, 159–160
Humble, self-confident leaders, 33
Humility, genuine. See Genuine humility
Hunger, One Acre Fund and ending cycle
    of, 186, 188, 189, 197

IBM, 74
Ice Bucket Challenge, 177
Incentives, becoming a best investment
    and, 160–163
Inclusive leadership, at Ernst & Young, 145

Infighting, 52

Innovation, best partnerships and promotion of, 121–123

"Intellectual-agility" approach, to talent development, 146–147

Interest rate environment, bank revenue and, 156–157

Internal network, importance of, 147

Inventory carrying costs, 159

Inventory management, cash flow and, 158

Investment capital:
alpha-performing companies and, 164
competition for, 132

Investor point-of-view, private equity firms and, 163–166

Jacobs, Don, 4

Jealousy, teams and, 50

Job losses, self-reflection and, 24

Johnson & Johnson, 87

Kenya, One Acre Fund and farm families in, 186, 187, 188, 195

Kramer, Mark, 75, 169, 184

Last Hunger Season, The (Thurow), 189

Layoffs, 148

Leaders:
best teams and, 51–52
genuinely humble, 44–45
lack of self-reflection among, 58, 59
management by walking around and, 64–65
turnaround, 70–72

Leadership:
followership and, 36
self-reflection and business orientation of, 19–20
true self-confidence and, 40–41

Leader's values, start-up companies and, 74–77

Leader-team engagement, best teams and, 65

Leading up, 25–27

Lehman Brothers, bankruptcy of, 155

Loan transactions, One Acre model and, 193

Local culture, organizational culture and, 145

Long-term partnerships, earning, 100–102

Lou Gehrig's Disease, Ice Bucket Challenge and, 177

Loyalty, 83, 135–136

Luck, success and, 46

Macho group, false self-confidence and, 36

Madison Dearborn Partners, 12, 41, 86, 87, 114, 133, 154, 163–164

Mail-order pharmacies, Catamaran Corporation and, 118

Management by walking around, 64–65

Margin, cash flow and, 159

Market capitalization, Northern Trust, 161

Market facilitation, One Acre model and, 193–194

Market intelligence, best partners and, 99–100

Marketplace returns, Campbell Soup Company turnaround and, 69–70

Marriage, true partnership and, 101–102

MasterCard Foundation, 195

Mayo Clinic model, description of, 108

McKinsey & Company, 78

Meaning, values-based leadership and, 191

Mergers, 59
between best partners, 95
cross-border, 125

Microloans, One Acre model and, 193

Minority students, graduation rate for, 181

Money-market funds, 157

Morale, best talent and, 149

Morrison, Denise, 70

Motorola, downfall at, 56–57

Motorola Mobility, 57

Motorola Solutions, 57

Mutual commitment, best partnership and, 102

Natural resource usage, shared value and, 184

Neaman, Mark R., 19, 103, 104, 105, 106, 108, 109, 110, 111

Negative events, self-reflection and, 21, 24

Nongovernmental organizations (NGOs), 168

Nonprofit organizations:
best citizenship and, 174
best investments and, 132

Northern Trust Corporation, 44, 45, 154
employee-shareholder alignment at, 160–161
market capitalization of, 133, 161
Quarter Century Club, 161
shareholder value and doing the right thing at, 154–157

NorthShore University HealthSystem, 19, 94–95, 100
Cardinal Health partnership with, 110
collaboration in action, 102–106
electronic medical records system for, 104, 105, 106, 107, 109, 110

Epic Systems Corporation collaboration with, 104–106, 109, 110
health care delivery within, 103
high level consistent performance at, 103–104
long-term relationships and, 103–104
physician best partnership and, 108, 109
University of Chicago Pritzker School of Medicine partnership with, 109–111
Northwestern University, Kellogg School of Management, 12, 93, 148, 169, 171–172, 185

One Acre Fund, 9, 169, 185
ethos of giving and, 190–191
failures and lessons learned at, 195–196
farm families served per year by, 186–187
finding meaning through involvement with, 191–192
five bests in action and, 197–199
funding sources for, 194–195
putting farmers first through, 188–189
One Acre model, steps in, 192–194
Operating expenses, cash flow and, 159–160
Operations management, cash flow and, 158
Opinions, answers vs., 29
Organic growth, 123
Organizational accountability, 131
Organizations:
best-investment, 146
as best partners, 91–92
strong cultural alignment across, 144
Osborn, William, 156
Out-of-the-box thinking, best teams and, 84–85
Overpayment, failed acquisitions and, 124
Ownership in start-ups, attitude and, 84

Paralysis by analysis, 29
Park, Jeff, 122
PBM. See Pharmacy benefit manager
Peer-to-peer marketing, viral, 177
Pension funds, 163
"People agenda," setting at Ernst & Young, 139–140
Performance:
best partnerships and, 103–104
best teams and, 62
Performance reviews, 136
Personal capital, 132
Perspective, 41. See also Balance
best investments and, 133
customer best partnerships and, 115
self-reflection and, 28–30

start-up companies and, 83
Peters, Tom, 64
Pharmaceutical supply chain, Catamaran Corporation and, 118
Pharmacy benefit manager, 118, 120, 121, 122, 123
Philanthropy, 175
ethos of giving and, 189–191
profits and, 173
Target Corporation and legacy of, 168, 172, 178–182
Physician best partnership, NorthShore University HealthSystem and, 108, 109
Points of Light Institute, Campbell Soup Company employee volunteerism and, 69–70
Porter, Michael, 75, 169, 184
Post-mortem, pre-mortem vs., 85
Poverty, One Acre Fund and alleviation of, 186, 188–189, 190, 197, 198
Powell, Alma, 181
Powell, Colin, 181
Pre-mortem, post-mortem vs., 85
Prescription drugs, Catamaran Corporation business model and, 120–121
Prescriptive analytics, 119
Prescriptive data modeling, 119
Pressure, eliminating, 20–23
Prices and pricing:
best partnerships and, 110–111
shareholder value and, 159
Price-to-earnings (P/E) ratio, 157
Priorities, identifying through self-reflection, 18
Private equity firms, investor point-of-view and, 163–166
Productivity, Campbell Soup Company turnaround and, 67
Professional services firms, 137
intellectual agility at, 146
Profits and profitability:
downsizing and increase in, 135
philanthropy and, 173
Publicly traded companies, best investments and, 132
Purpose-driven companies, 172

Qualitative metrics, 165
Quinnox, 78

Receivables, cash flow and, 158
Reference checking, 79
Remembering the cube concept, genuine humility and, 43
Reorganizations, 148

Reputation Institute, Campbell Soup
   Company turnaround and, 69
Resources, stewardship of, 135
Respect:
   best teams and, 51
   genuine humility and, 42
Return on investment:
   Campbell Soup Company turnaround
      and, 68
   organizations of all types and, 131, 132,
      135
Rewards, for best teams, 87–88
Right sizing, 148
Risk, entrepreneur's values and, 76–77
Rwanda, One Acre Fund and farm families
   in, 186, 195

SaaS. *See* Software as a service
Salaries, cash flow and, 158
Sales:
   cash flow and, 158
   shareholder value and, 159
SAP, Fieldglass purchased by, 20, 77, 78, 86,
   88
Schools, Target Corporation's focus on,
   180–182
Schwab Foundation, 195
Self-awareness, 2, 13, 31, 197
   best citizenship and, 183
   self-reflection as gateway to, 16, 17, 19
   values-based leaders and, 11
Self-confidence, false, 35–37
Self-confidence, true. *See* True self-
   confidence
Self-knowledge, 2, 3, 13
   best citizenship and, 183
   self-reflection as gateway to, 16
   values-based leaders and, 11, 13
Self-reflection, 1, 2–3, 5, 9, 13, 41, 167, 174
   acquisitions and, 125, 126
   in action, 197
   balance and perspective and, 28–30,
      31–32
   best citizenship and, 169, 177, 180, 183
   best investments and, 133, 149–150, 166
   best partners and, 92, 97
   best teams and, 49
   business orientation of leadership and,
      19–20
   business transformation and, 123
   centering your best self and, 22–23
   eliminating worry, fear, anxiety, pressure,
      and stress through, 20–23
   employing, values-based leaders and, 48
   entrepreneurs and, 75, 76
   function of, 15

genuine humility and, 42
importance of, 16–18
leaders who don't engage in, 58, 59
leading up and, 25–27
pausing for, 27–28
true self-confidence and, 36
turnaround leaders and, 71
values and priorities discovered through,
   199
values-based leaders and, 11
Self-reflective behavior, modeling for your
   team, 24–25
Servant leaders, 80, 137, 196
Shared value:
   best citizenship, community alignment,
      and, 184
   defined, 175
   reinventing business agenda and, 169
   understanding, 176
Shareholder return:
   best investment and, 133
   doing good and, 172
Shareholders, 131
Shareholder value. *See also* Total
      shareholder return
   building, by doing the right thing,
      154–157
   parts of, 152
   sales and, 159
   talent and, 148, 149
   tying incentives to best investment and,
      160–163
Shekhawat, Jai, 19, 53, 77, 78, 79, 80, 81, 82,
   83, 84, 85, 86, 87
Silo mentalities, discouraging, values-based
   organizations and, 146, 158–159, 160
Skills, success and factors beyond, 45, 46
Smallholder farmers, One Acre model and,
   192
Socially responsible investing, 175
Social media, 30
Social responsibility, 6, 8, 168, 169, 174, 179
   Campbell Soup Company turnaround
      and, 69–70
   empowered teams and, 182–183
Societal progress, shared value and, 184
Soft metrics, 166
Software as a service, 84
Sovereign wealth funds, 163
Specialization, 146
Specialty pharmacies, Catamaran
   Corporation and, 118
Spiritual perspective, success and, 46
S&P Packaged Foods index, 69
Stakeholders, earning returning for, 131
Start-up companies:

best teams and, 52, 88–89
competitive advantage with, 97–98
from launch to scale, 82–84
leader's values and, 74–77
lean, 73
out-of-the-box thinking at, 84–85
recruiting people for, 77
Steward leader, 7
Stock appreciation, 152
Stock options, 160
Stock prices:
    acquisitions and, 163
    education of shareholders and, 162
    operating expenses and, 159–160
    philanthropic giving and, 173
Strategic partnerships, building on,
    106–109
Stress:
    eliminating, 20–23
    lack of self-reflection and, 28
Success:
    best team and, 53
    factors beyond hard work and skills in,
    45–46
    success building on, 109–111
Sullivan, Tim, 133, 154, 164, 165, 166
Suppliers as best partners. *See also*
    NorthShore University HealthSystem
    competitive pressures and, 99–100
    earned long-term partnerships and,
    100–102
    in holistic relationship, 97–111
    partnerships built on partnerships and,
    106–109
    pursuit of excellence and, 111
    success built on success and, 109–111
Supply chain, human element in, 117–118
Sustainability, 175, 178
Sustainable farming, Campbell Soup
    Company turnaround and, 69
Sustainable organizations, talent
    development and, 149–150
SXC Health Solutions, 119, 120, 122, 123,
    127, 128. *See also* Catamaran
    Corporation
Syntel, 78

Take Charge of Education program
    (Target), 180
Talent, 131, 133, 158
    balance and development of, 138
    best investment in, 135–150, 164
    culture and, 140–145
    developing, 144–146
    financial performance and link with, 150
    getting priorities right with, 137–139

intellectual agility and development of,
    146–147
management, importance of, 149
morale and, 149
Tanzania, One Acre Fund and farm families
    in, 186
Target Corporation, 190
    education initiatives of, 180–182
    integrated approach to best citizenship
    at, 183
    leading with a purpose at, 178–180
    legacy of philanthropy at, 168, 172, 178,
    179–182
    team-member empowerment at, 179
Team-mindset, best-investment perspective
    on, 147–150
Teams, 147, 148. *See also* Best team
    acknowledging significant contributions
    of, 64
    as co-contributors to greater whole, 48
    genuine humility and contributions of, 42
    leaders with true self-confidence and, 41
    meaning infused into work of, 191, 192
    success and, 46
    Target Corporation and development of,
    179
Technology, pharmacy business and, 119
Tesla, 73
Thielen, Rob, 174
Thierer, Mark, 79, 118, 119, 120, 121, 122,
    127, 128, 129
Thompson, Leigh, 93
Thurow, Roger, 189
Timing, success and, 46
Top-line growth, 136
Total shareholder returns, 69, 152, 153,
    158, 160. *See also* Shareholder value
Toxic environments, 55
Toys for Tots, 177
Transaction bonuses, at Fieldglass, 87
Tropical disease initiatives, 197
True self-confidence, 1, 3, 5, 7, 9, 13–14, 33,
    35–37, 98, 126, 167, 180
    in action, 197
    admitting when you are wrong and, 39–40
    best partners and, 92
    best teams and, 49
    entrepreneurship and, 81
    leadership and, 40–41
    leading up and, 27
    in real world, 47–48
    turnaround leaders and, 71
    two-question test and, 37–39
    values-based leaders and, 11, 48
    what I know and what I don't know,
    34–35, 37

Trust, best team and, 63, 65
Truth about Negotiations, The (Thompson), 93
TSRs. *See* Total shareholder returns
Turf wars, 59
Turnaround leaders, 70–72

University of Chicago Pritzker School of Medicine, NorthShore University HealthSystem partnership with, 109–111
Unsatisfied customers, depleting emotional bank account of organization and, 66
USAID, 195

Valuation metric, 165
Value-based culture, best investment and, 140
Value chain, customer best partnerships and focus on, 115–117, 129
Values-based culture, best citizenship and, 183–184, 192
Values-based leaders, 81
   best citizenship and, 182
   of best teams, 51–52
   defined, 11
   mission of, 8
Values-based leadership, 16, 166, 167, 168, 171, 173. *See also* Balance; Genuine humility; True self-confidence
   alpha and, 164
   best citizenship in action and, 198–199
   best partners and, 92
   continuous, self-reflective nature of, 199
   customer best partnerships and, 115
   foundations of, 5
   four principles of, 13, 14
   One Acre Fund and, 187
   shareholder value and, 154, 155
   total shareholder return and, 153

turnaround leaders and, 71
Values-based leadership journey, doing well by doing good and, 184
Values-based organizations:
   consistency established within, 61
   mission of, 8
Values-based principles, organizations lacking foundation of, 55
Values-driven individuals, 168
Vendor management system, cloud-based, at Fieldglass, 77, 78
Verizon Wireless, 87
VMS. *See* Vendor management system
Volunteerism:
   Campbell Soup Company turnaround and:, 69–70
   Target Corporation's empowered teams and, 183

Waddell, Rick, 44, 45, 133, 154, 155, 156, 157, 161
Walking around, management by, 64–65
Wandering around, 64
Ward, Laysha, 172, 178, 179, 180, 181, 182, 183
Washington Post, 181
Women, Campbell Soup Company and expanded opportunities for, 69
Worker safety, shared value and, 184
Workplace environment, Campbell Soup Company turnaround and, 69–70
World Bank, 197
World Economic Forum, 195, 196
Worry:
   eliminating, 20–23
   lack of self-reflection and, 28
WSJ. Magazine, 34

Youn, Andrew, 9, 169, 185, 186, 190, 191, 192, 193, 194, 195, 196, 197, 198, 199